'Pete Atkinson's telling  the Bible is a fascinat poetic imagination give and hearts of the many explores the anger and Trinity as the people of God respond to God's overtures of love and his desire for an intimate relationship with his people. We ride the roller coaster with biblical characters as they walk closely and faithfully with God for a while, walk away in fear and rebellion and then return in repentance and faith. The tensions between sovereignty and responsibility, justice and mercy, and the discipline and delight of God in relation to his people are powerfully conveyed. We are caught up in the amazing drama and strong emotions of the story. I have been a believer for many years and I found it hard to put down this dramatic summary and retelling of the story. It helped me, in a new way, to connect my story with the larger biblical story of redemption.'

Dr Richard Winter, Professor Emeritus of Practical Theology at Covenant Theological Seminary

'Dramatic. Lively. Well-informed. Whether used as a script for public performance or read privately, its vitality will engage. You'll learn the individual stories, their setting and the big story all at the same time. I enjoyed reading this book and I'm sure you will too.'

Dr Derek Tidball, Former Principal of London School of Theology and Former President of the Baptist Union

For Bethany, Jacob and Oliver

THE RESCUE MISSION

The Bible As We've
Never Experienced It Before

We enter not knowing what to expect.
We lay down all preconceptions, all prior knowledge.
We choose to enter with an open mind.

0.00 – Order to Chaos

Tears cascade incessantly from the bloodshot, pain-stained eyes of three friends huddled together. Mourning their loss, with arms wrapped around each other, all cry out in agony.

Together this intimate embrace forms a creative community of love called Elohim, where joy and affection find their home. If only the trio had maintained their focus within their embracing circle of paradise, there would be no tears falling today. But Love by its very nature looks outward. And the view breaks Elohim's heart.

Everywhere hatred glares back.

Everywhere suffering permeates.

Everywhere every thought is evil.[1]

Holding hands tightly, faces flooded with tears, hearts *filled with pain*,[2] Elohim grieves. Hope has died. Their nature - their community of paradise - is incompatible with the torture-scarred landscape. There can be no relationship.

With the outlook so bleak, Love is left with only one option.

Gripping each other ever closer, the three whisper their united conclusion: *'I will destroy all human beings that I made on the earth...'*

Their voices break down, choking and trembling under the weight of emotion. The sounds of sobbing are eventually accompanied by further strained words.

'...because I am sorry I have made them.'[3]
The decision is definite.
Elohim has chosen.
Humans will suffer no more.
Because all humans will be destroyed.
Mourning their loss, tears fall like raindrops, flooding the entire earth.

This devastating conclusion couldn't be more different from the one originally dreamt of, envisioned, and sculpted by Elohim.

In the beginning,[4] out of love, passion and desire for relationship, the heavens and the earth took form in spectacular fashion, bringing order to chaos. *'Let us make human beings in our image and likeness,'*[5] the three lovers leapt enthusiastically, overjoyed at the prospect of sharing their nature with the centrepiece of their creation. Having provided for their every need, the breath of Elohim rushed through man and woman, releasing life.

Everywhere Elohim looked, the completed work of art shone with excellence.[6] The Artists smiled expansively with the utmost pride and satisfaction.

Full of joy, there was no pain.
Full of love, there was no shame.[7]
Full of life, there was no death.

Of all the great gifts showered upon the first humans, the greatest was freedom. Free to roam and explore however they wished, the possibilities seemed limitless. And the most incredible opportunity of all was residing in the company of their Creator, living in intimacy with the breath that brought them life; the very Breath within their lungs. Created by Love, for love, to love, the relationship would fulfil the deepest desires of Elohim's heart.

But relationships can never be forced.

Love must be freely chosen.

Love must be freely reciprocated.

Which is why, *in the middle of the garden*[8] - planted at the heart of Elohim's artwork - there stood two trees.

One tree was called Life.

Fruit from the other tree brought Death.

'You may eat the fruit from any tree,' Love explained. *'But you must not eat the fruit from the tree which gives the knowledge of good and evil. If you ever eat fruit from that tree, you will die!'*[9]

Vulnerable, with heart flung out on the line, pure, perfect Love could do no more than cry out 'Choose life!' and watch on transfixed, waiting for response.

Jaws dropped, trembling in horror.

When, into the scene, doubt descended.[10]

From order to chaos, clarity was distorted.

From the tree of knowledge, fruit was selected.

And from each eye, the first tears of rejection fell.

Choosing disconnection from their Designer, human elegance diminished. Yet still succulent fruit hung from the tree of life, ripe for picking. In their wounded state, humans could still eat the fruit of life and *live forever*.[11]

Doing so would leave them perpetually wounded.

Permanently diminished.

Disconnected… for ever.

The prospect was terrifying.

Acting quickly to avert an eternal catastrophe, from which there could have been no rescue, Elohim forced man and woman out from the garden and erected a spectacular security barrier *flashing back and forth to guard the way to the tree of life.*[12]

'Far from home,' a tender voice recalls, 'having never previously worked to survive, the daily necessities of life became a constant challenge. Within a generation, frustration fed jealousy and anger. Then murder.[13] Spilt blood cried out from the ground,[14] contaminating our lush handiwork, staining and stifling, rendering it sterile.'

'In an attempt to end the bloodshed,' sighs a second wistful voice, 'I told the first murderer, Cain, "*If anyone kills you, I will punish that person seven times more.*"[15] I hoped the warning would discourage revenge attacks. But within five generations, Lamech boasted, "*I killed a man for wounding me, a young man for hitting me. If Cain's killer is punished seven times, then Lamech's killer will be punished seventy seven times.*"[16]

Love's lament pauses - hanging in the agony - before continuing, 'Oh, how I dream of one day teaching humans to forgive not *seven times, but seventy seven times.*'[17]

'But I can live within humans no longer,' a third voice interjects, heartbroken. 'The extremity of human dirt has smothered their beauty, making us incompatible. My Breath will leave their flesh, and *they will live only one hundred and twenty years.*'[18]

Death.

Death has arrived.

Mourning their loss, tears fall like raindrops flooding the entire earth.

1.   Genesis 6:5
2.   Genesis 6:6
3.   Genesis 6:7
4.   Genesis 1:1
5.   Genesis 1:26
6.   Genesis 1:31
7.   Genesis 2:25
8.   Genesis 2:9 (NIV)
9.   Genesis 2:16–17
10. Genesis 3:1
11. Genesis 3:22
12. Genesis 3:24 (NIV)
13. Genesis 4:8
14. Genesis 4:10
15. Genesis 4:15
16. Genesis 4:24
17. Matthew 18:22
18. Genesis 6:3

0.01 – We Choose To Enter

Many times before we have walked past this locked, dilapidated building and looked back with disdain, relieved to live in a more aware, more advanced era. This throwback to an ancient way of life had simply left a blotch on today's landscape.

But occasionally - just occasionally - the dull, discoloured concrete and smashed windows have appealed to our inquisitive nature. Every now and again, we have stopped to wonder whether this derelict eyesore contained any discarded treasures.

Today, the gates are open.

Today, it's as if the building is ushering us in.

So we enter not knowing what to expect.

We lay down all preconceptions, all prior knowledge.

We choose to enter with an open mind.

Our heart thumps as we clamber through the debris spread chaotically across the floor. Occasionally we stop to inspect objects of interest, before a door in the distance catches our eye. Sunbeams reflect off a silver, metallic plaque. The door is rugged and stripped down, and engraved into the plaque are the words: 'Rescue Headquarters.'

Captivated by intrigue, we push open the door.

'Are we ready to do this?' a voice from Elohim asks.

'Just look at Noah's beauty,' another responds.

'Suffering may saturate every life but this is not a lost cause. Our characteristics have not disappeared completely. In Noah there is hope. In Noah there is inspiration.[1] Starting with Noah our character can spread out across the globe, overwhelming all hatred. Love can win out.'

'Love is always a risk,' adds a third besotted voice. 'And we love too much not to. Love always opens itself up to the possibility of rejection. It's the only way. The agony of heartbreak will be worth it for the joy of acceptance, the euphoria of relationship.'

'Humans can be beautiful again. Restored to full splendour, they could once again access the tree of life.[2] They would become eternally attractive,[3] and we would walk with them again, in even greater, limitless intimacy.'

'Oh, it will be glorious. I cannot contain my anticipation. My heart leaps with excitement.' The voice pauses, taking a deep breath. 'I would be willing to die for that.'[4]

'So we are agreed then?'

'Yes.'

'Yes, let's do it.'

'Let our Rescue Mission begin.'

---

1. Genesis 6:8-9
2. 2 Timothy 1:9-10
3. Titus 1:2
4. Acts 2:23

PHASE ONE

1.01 – A New Beginning

With just one foot inside the room we are instantly amazed. Besides bookshelves and a desk, this is no ordinary office. Every square inch of the room's four walls is decorated with paper and card, all filled with detailed text, diagrams and illustrations.

Mesmerised, we don't even notice the door close behind us.[1] Instead we rock back on our heels, and look up then down, left then right, in an attempt to take it all in. The extent of the information is simply overwhelming. Of one thing we are sure: this 'Headquarters' must be the hub of a substantial, strategic operation.

But before we can contemplate the terrifying prospect of stumbling across a secret criminal lair, we stand gripped by text to our left. On the posters nearest to the entrance, beneath a prominent 'Phase One' heading, a mysterious narrative begins.

From the sanctuary of an undercover decking, a drained and bedraggled figure stands watching the rain drive down and bounce high off the bobbing surface. Looking out over the waters, the woman picks out a single mutilated carcass rotting among the masses below. Was this mangled mess once human? It is too difficult to tell now.

Starving and sleep-deprived, every night this woman lies haunted by the shrieks, the final cries of the massacred; friends and strangers alike flung through the air, flailing, gasping, pulled under, never to be seen again. They didn't stand a chance. *Even the highest mountains* were submerged.[2]

Every night, she lies weeping, grieving, besieged by the memories, beset with regret that no one had listened; that no one had sought sanctuary on board her enormous, spacious ship.[3]

For most people, the torment would paralyse both body and mind. But not this courageous woman. Ploughing through her pain, every new morning she reminds herself that she is privileged.

Precious.

Significant.

She is the mother of the only family left alive.

Every new morning, the experienced matriarch finds fresh motivation in the bright burning love of her three sons, their wives, and of course Noah, her brave yet tender hero. Though he had appeared insane, though he had been abused and ridiculed, supporting her man on his mission was the best decision she ever made. Without Noah's expert craftsmanship she would not be here now. She would be adding negligible weight to the mass of meat and bones being tossed about by the waves.

Her skin crawling, Noah's wife is lost in a haze of

thoughts when a shout reverberates through the ship.

'It's stopped! It's stopped!'

Her head jolts.

Could it be true?

The eyes focus.

A myriad of circles no longer dance across the rocking waves.

Vertical streaks no longer flash furiously.

She holds out a hand.

The palm remains dry.

A skip, a hop, a dance - her sprint has it all. Arms flinging chaotically, she runs like one of her ship's galloping creatures, head first into the hysterical embrace of her family.

Thoroughly transfixed, the Lovers of Elohim brush away the final tears from their eyes. Prior to Love's devastating deluge, every human thought was evil. Now, for the first time in centuries, humans are feeling joy; pure, undiluted joy. Here, in the jubilation of Noah's family, Elohim sees the first shoots of hope, the first flowering buds rising from the flood, the first olive branch of rejuvenated life.[4]

'*Grow in number and fill the earth,*'[5] the enveloping trio cheer in optimistic unison. It's the second time that creation has heard this command to co-create. Despite the disastrous results last time, Love is giving humanity a second chance to thrive.

'*I will demand the life of anyone who takes another person's life,*'[6] Elohim insists, desperate to cut down the disproportionate revenge attacks which previously spiralled out of control.

The choice remains.

To love or to hate?

To flourish or flounder?

To develop or destroy?

Humanity's capacity for violence remains a distinct possibility. Love may one day be grieved to the point of destruction again.

Which prompts the first covenant.

An agreement.

A promise.

A contract.

Love's covenant with the whole world will place a marker in the ground, signposting a critical, irreversible choice. The decision will stand firm and true throughout the entire Rescue Mission.

'I now establish my covenant with you and with your descendants after you,' Elohim announces with great passion. *'Never again will there be a flood to destroy the earth… I have set my rainbow in the clouds, and it will be the sign of the covenant between me and the earth.'*[7]

The promise is unconditional. Even if humans tarnish themselves just as severely as they did before, even if every thought becomes evil again, Love will not give up. The Community of Elohim is in this for the long haul, fully committed, no matter the cost. In no disillusionment as to the scale of the challenge, knowing that *their thoughts are evil even when they are young,*[8] the Creator has chosen to never stop believing in the fundamental goodness of his artwork. This is a new beginning, and God has faith that his beauty will ultimately win out.

Noah lies naked, drunk out of his mind.[9]
The next morning, still hung over, the one man worth saving fires a curse upon his grandson,[10] staining Canaan's descendants for generations to come.

1. Genesis 7:16
2. Genesis 7:19
3. Genesis 6:15
4. Genesis 8:11
5. Genesis 9:1
6. Genesis 9:5
7. Genesis 9:9–13 (NIV)
8. Genesis 8:21
9. Genesis 9:21
10. Genesis 9:25

PHASE TWO

2.01 – We Will Give Birth

Deep in thought, three friends look down upon a large chart, full of painted text, arrows and illustrations.

'Several nations have formed,' notes the first Strategist. 'With varying languages.'

'Fuelling confusion and suspicion.'[1]

'Furthering violence and division.'

'So here's the plan: we will give birth to our own nation.'

'A nation who will promote our values.'

'A nation who will *live right and be fair.*'[2]

'A nation who will inspire and attract others towards creating a greater, healthier world.'

'Our pioneering nation shall own the land currently inhabited by those Noah cursed; that way, our blessing shall overcome the curse. And through blessing our nation, all *the people on earth will be blessed.*'[3]

'But to blaze with our beauty, our nation must first absorb our beauty. To illuminate Love, they must know our Love.'

'And choose our Love.'

'Like Noah building his ship, our plans require co-operation.'

'I wonder, Abba, how will Abram respond?'

A frustrated kick to the ground sends a cloud of dust puffing up into Abram's face. Sighing indignantly, the wanderer shakes his head, flicking dirt back into the air. Drought after drought, famine after famine, Abram and his wife are forced to frequently uproot their lives in search of fertile land. Despite being *rich in cattle, silver and gold*,[4] the couple's nomadic existence is worlds apart from the prosperity and security they once enjoyed in the great city of Ur.

Riddled with resentment, desperate to clear his jumbled mind, Abram walks aimlessly, dragging his feet through Canaan's hostile sands. Nearly a decade has passed since he heard the promises that brought him to these barren plains.[5]

All these years on, nothing has changed.

Not one promise has materialised.

More recently, Abram was told, *'Look all around you… All this land that you see I will give to you and your descendants.'*[6] The voice was just too definite to doubt. Yet the very mention of descendants makes Abram feel sick.

Sarai, his wife, is infertile.[7]

And in a society where family ties bring status, the shame is relentless. For decades, Abram and Sarai have fought their grief, finding comfort in each other, coming to terms with their tragic, irreparable void. Elohim's recent promises simply opened the wounds again.

With evening drawing in, Abram arrives home to find his tent empty. Exhausted, he falls to the ground in a crumpled heap.

'Abram, don't be afraid.'

Digging his head further into bent knees, Abram strains to stifle a tired, aggravated groan.

'Abram, I will defend you, and I will give you a great reward.'[8]

With tears welling in his eyes, his cheeks burning, Abram can hold it in no longer. The question which incessantly pounds within is finally let fly.

'What can you give me? I have no son, so my slave... will get everything I own after I die.'[9]

'You will have a son of your own.'[10]

Love's adamant tone carries with it great tenderness.

'There are so many stars you cannot count them,' Elohim explains, ushering Abram outside. *'Your descendants also will be too many to count.'*[11]

Staring into the expansive depths, slowly but surely Abram's cheeks lighten. A satisfied smile stretches wide. The awesome sight is evidence enough: the Architect of such beauty is surely capable of blessing him with a child.[12]

'Abram, Abram, where are you?'

Abram freezes. Sarai is home: what should he say?

'I'm out here, my love.'

Feeling his wife's arms squeezing around his waist, playfully swaying him from side to side, feeling her great affection, tears begin to roll down Abram's cheeks.

'What is it, love?' Sarai whispers, stroking her fingers reassuringly through his hair. 'You can tell me.'

Abram turns to look far into his wife's eyes. 'God met me again. I will... I will be a father.'

Sarai looks away, humiliation hanging from her face.

'God *has kept me from having children.*'[13]

Sharing her pain, Abram embraces his wife.

'I know, I know.'

Clearing away the teardrops from her blurred vision, Sarai looks up again into Abram's eyes. Though each word hurts considerably, she speaks with clarity: '*Go, sleep with my maidservant; perhaps I can build a family through her.*'[14]

1. Genesis 11:9
2. Genesis 18:19
3. Genesis 12:3
4. Genesis 13:2
5. Genesis 12:1
6. Genesis 13:14–15
7. Genesis 11:30
8. Genesis 15:1
9. Genesis 15:2
10. Genesis 15:4
11. Genesis 15:5
12. Genesis 15:6
13. Genesis 16:2 (NIV)
14. Genesis 16:2 (NIV)

2.02 - Out of Love

The discomfort in our gut is sharp.

God wants his nation to demonstrate love.

Surely, he wants it to be born out of love, doesn't he?

Not a one-night stand.

Alongside the Headquarters' written narratives, there are hundreds of interweaving arrows, jottings and sketches, forming an intricate, complex web. Some markings have been written in paint and pen. Others have been written in pencil. Others have been crossed out. Some pencil markings have been traced over in pen.

To what extent, we wonder, will things happen as the Rescue Strategists intend; as they desire?

Abram can sleep with Sarai.

Or Abram can sleep with Sarai's servant.

The choice is his.

Love can instruct.

Love can inspire.

Love can woo.

But Love cannot - Love will not - control.

In pencil, our eyes glimpse the name 'Ishmael': Abram's child born of Hagar, Sarai's maidservant.[1] But standing out bright and bold on the wall - written in indelible ink - we discover a second, crucial, future defining covenant. To mark the occasion of Ishmael's thirteenth birthday - his coming of age - the Community of Elohim promises, *'I will be your God and the God of all your descendants.'*[2]

Abram's family shall be God's family.

Elohim shall be their Father.

Nurturing, maturing; drawing out their beauty.

So important, so foundational, the promise must never be forgotten. Which is why, from now on, Abram will be known as Abraham, meaning 'father of many.'

What's more, under the agreement, every male belonging to Elohim must be cut by a knife, marked by circumcision, as a constant, physical reminder of where the whole community's identity lies - a constant reminder of how precious, how treasured every child of God is.

At last, Abraham can rest and relax. Assured of a tremendous legacy, he sighs and smiles, then shuts his eyes, soaking in the prospect of his wild and boisterous Ishmael[3] enjoying intimacy with Elohim.

'I will change the name of Sarai, your wife, to Sarah.'[4]

Abraham's eyes open, surprised and alert.

'I will bless her,' Elohim continues, *'and give her a son, and you will be the father.'*[5]

As if tripped by a wire, Abraham's knees buckle forward and his face crashes into the dust. The very words he's longed to hear all his life: at first, a burst of ecstasy fills his stomach; then his laughter slows, the sound nervous and disturbing.

'Please let Ishmael be the son you promised,'[6] the father begs with teeth clenched. *'Can a man have a child when he is one hundred?'* Abraham's gasp is almost

inaudible.

'Can Sarah give birth... when she is ninety?'[7]

Though no one is around to hear it, we immediately regret the laughter which slips out.[8] But then again, why shouldn't we laugh? Sarah is simply too old to have a child. Even if she did conceive, she would surely die in labour.

Vacant and numb, drained of all joy, an ageing father rises silently under the starry night. Striding stiff-lipped, fighting back the tears, Abraham watches his beloved Isaac - his precious, promised son - following obediently; obliviously.

After three days trekking and climbing, the pair reach their mountainous destination. An altar of wood is prepared, before - pale faced and stony eyed - Abraham grabs hold of his unsuspecting son.

Born miraculously.

Out of love.

Sarah's son Isaac was all set to inherit a glorious, prosperous future, in an unbreakable, everlasting, indelible covenant.[9]

Was it all a con? A sick, sadistic, meaningless game?

Because Elohim's cry was unmistakable: *'Take Isaac, the son you love, and go to the land of Moriah. Kill him there and offer him as a burnt offering.'*[10]

Is this revenge for sleeping with Hagar?

Cruel, cold-hearted comeuppance?

Abraham sharpens his blade.

Sweat forms on our brow.
Has God given up?
How could Love possibly want this?

The knife draws back, rising high over Isaac, poised to
strike a deadly blow.

1. Genesis 16:4
2. Genesis 17:7
3. Genesis 16:12
4. Genesis 17:15
5. Genesis 17:16
6. Genesis 17:18
7. Genesis 17:17
8. Genesis 21:6
9. Genesis 17:19 (NIV)
10. Genesis 22:1-2

2.03 – Collision is Coming

Unified in their pain, united in their resolve, the all-consuming, all-encompassing, all-embracing Elohim hovers over Abraham and Isaac, acutely aware of a deeply-rooted anxiety ricocheting within every human.

Too much rain, all life is submerged.

Too little rain, all life soon withers.

Staring at the skies in helpless terror, Love's cherished creation began to wonder whether something had gone horribly wrong. These forces beyond human control: are they furious?

Vengeful?

Malevolent?

Or is their rage reversible?

Would devotion appease?

Would gifts win favour?

As desperation intensified, humanity's offerings became increasingly extreme; increasingly costly; increasingly bloody.

Some even offered the greatest sacrifice of all.

They killed their firstborn child.

'Abraham! Abraham!'[1] Elohim roars.

His knife still airborne, the father freezes. Eyes clenched tight, pain pulsates through his pounding heart.

'Don't kill your son or hurt him in any way.'[2]

The left eye opens first, then the right. His muscles relax, his racing heart slows. As his raised arm drops safely to his side, Abraham wraps himself tight around Isaac's distressed, shaking frame. Relieved beyond measure, tears surge.

And in the most dramatic way possible, the Lovers of Elohim have made their point. The creator and controller of the elements does not demand human sacrifices.

Love shudders at the sight of spilt human blood.

The killing of children leaves Love totally repulsed.

Looking up from his trembling son, Abraham glimpses a ram caught in a thorny bush. 'The ram shall take your place,' he whispers tenderly into his son's ear, running his hands through Isaac's hair.

'Oh, Abraham, precious Abraham,' weeps a voice from Elohim. 'I shall never forget how - even before tying up his son - he reassured Isaac, '"*God himself will provide the lamb for the burnt offering.*"'[3]

'Abba, Abraham's remarkable words reach out to the very core of our Rescue Mission.'

'Yes, in the same locality as Abraham's offering, we will provide.'

'We will offer the greatest sacrifice of all.'

Moving fast, desperate to put ground between himself and his enraged pursuer, Jacob anxiously pushes onwards. Focussed as he is, running for his life, the runaway hardly notices the setting sun until darkness has engulfed and he can go no further. Gasping for breath, Jacob is forced to rest.

In all his life, the quiet introvert has rarely ventured far from the family tents.[4] Tonight, he will sleep homeless and alone. And after what Jacob has just stolen, he is unlikely to ever return home in peace.

If he had just been born a few moments earlier, it wouldn't have come to this; Jacob wouldn't have been forced to such devious depths. It's utterly insane that his twin brother Esau should inherit God's monumental covenant with Abraham, while Jacob got nothing. Older than Jacob by minutes, Esau's descendants would be as many as the dust of the earth. Cold and afraid, the runaway rests his head on a stone and before long, his mind seamlessly slips into a curious alternate reality.

In his dream, Jacob sees a ladder reaching from earth up into heaven,[5] directly connecting humanity with the home of a divine power.

This revolutionary image challenges and contradicts the widespread belief that the forces on which humans depend for life are disconnected.

Distant.

And disinterested.

By contrast, the God of Abraham and Isaac interacts personally, promising Jacob, *'Your descendants will be as many as the dust of the earth. All the families of the earth will be blessed through you.'*[6]

We stop in our tracks. This isn't right. Didn't it say that God's covenant with Abraham is continuing with

Esau? So why is he promising Jacob as many descendants as dust on the earth?

Jacob wakes to eerie silence, and in a flash, haunting memories flood his mind's eye. He recalls Esau, drawn and bedraggled, *almost dead from hunger*,[7] looking him in the eye and begging for food. Yet all Jacob saw was an opportunity. In exchange for a bowl of soup, he demanded, *'You must sell me your rights as the firstborn son.'*[8]

So selfish.

So heartless.

Then there's the con which fooled his father.

The con which roused his brother's vow to kill.[9]

Jacob lies stunned, struck by the thought of his blind and vulnerable father: so content, so accepting. Ever since his near-death experience as a child, Jacob's father Isaac has lived with 'God will provide' ingrained in his psyche. When his wife was unable to have children, Isaac had reason to believe that God could - and would - provide.[10]

For the rest of the night, Jacob stares out at the stars, wrestling with his shame. Slowly but surely, Elohim's promises gradually take root, enabling a healthy combination of humility and confidence to flourish. 'I *want God to be with me and to protect me,'* Jacob declares as a new day dawns. 'I want *to return in peace to my father's house.'*[11]

Two decades later, Jacob looks on in terror as an army

four hundred strong heads directly towards him.[12]

Leading the march is Esau.

Jacob gulps, draws breath then steps forward.

Falling flat on the ground, lying completely exposed, he peers up.

Esau is running right at him.

Collision is coming.

1. Genesis 22:11
2. Genesis 22:12
3. Genesis 22:8 (NIV)
4. Genesis 25:27
5. Genesis 28:12
6. Genesis 28:15
7. Genesis 25:32
8. Genesis 25:31
9. Genesis 27:41
10. Genesis 25:21
11. Genesis 28:20-21
12. Genesis 33:1

2.04 – Father's Arms

Linking hands in an explosion of celebration, forming a community of Love called Elohim, three friends dance in majestic unison at the sight of Esau wrapping his arms around Jacob and giving a delicate kiss.[1]

'Our image spreads, our love unites, our forgiveness restores,' Elohim sings in gloriously diverse tones, enamoured and enthralled by Esau's forgiveness-filled embrace. 'Yes, yes, it's happening!' the Community cheers in exquisite harmony as Jacob splutters to his brother, *'It is like seeing the face of God, because you have accepted me.'*[2]

'I'm creating some stories to encapsulate our aspirations,' reveals a buoyant voice. 'I want everyone to know that my Father's arms are outstretched. One story begins with a son rejecting his father's affection. And in Jacob and Esau's remarkable reconciliation I have found the climax: *While he was still a long way off, the father saw his son and was filled with compassion for him. So he ran to his son, threw his arms around him and kissed him.'*[3]

'My love, that is breathtaking.'

'Son, that is perfect.'

Wallowing in depression, a long drawn out groan leaves Jacob's mouth. Sometimes numb and empty, sometimes throbbing and sore, today's pain finds its root in times of great joy long ago, in the days when Jacob learnt to love. Falling head-over-heels for Rachel, a woman of stunning beauty,[4] Jacob quickly learnt the extent to which love requires sweat and sacrifice. He had to toil for many years before finally marrying his heart's desire.[5]

Knowing that his offspring would inherit astounding promises, Jacob soon discovered that - like his father and grandfather before him - his wife couldn't conceive. Instead, Jacob chose to father ten sons with three separate women.[6]

Each birth was simply wonderful.

But then came a day like no other.

Ensuring Phase Two would continue in a lineage of love, Elohim helped Rachel give birth to Joseph: Jacob's miracle son, born of his one true love.[7]

Which is why, when Esau's merciful arms later wrapped around, Jacob couldn't have been happier with life. After all the mistakes he had made, he felt abundantly blessed.

That was until the first tragedy struck.

Bringing life to her second child, Rachel didn't make it. The pain was too much.

She died in labour.[8]

Then came further devastation.

Aged seventeen, Joseph was out shepherding the flocks.

When a creature savagely attacked.

Mauling Joseph to pieces.[9]

As if that wasn't enough, now Jacob's family is

engulfed by famine. Far and wide, catastrophe is imminent. Soon the descendants of Abraham, the foundations of the Rescue Mission, will be no more.

Only one hope remains. Rumour has it that out in the west the respected Egyptians are selling an abundance of grain reserves to travellers from all over the earth. So Jacob has sent ten of his sons on a mission to Egypt. With his entire family's future.

Dependent on their success.[10]

Jacob turns to face his youngest son, the one he kept behind. The last remaining legacy of Rachel's love, Benjamin is to be protected at all costs. In Benjamin's warm eyes, Jacob sees Rachel's relentless compassion.

And Joseph's steadfast confidence.

Letting out another grating howl, Jacob closes his eyes and, like he has done so many times before, he tries to picture what Joseph would look like, all these years on. Having never found or buried his son's mutilated body, oh, how he longs for a shred of fiction in the account of Joseph's death.

The divine dancers of Elohim lean forward in anticipation as Jacob's ten sons wait in line to purchase grain from an Egyptian governor. Over the last decade, the devoted trio have helped this governor oversee the stockpiling of Egypt's reserves, single-handedly saving countless lives.

This governor has thrived in his rescuing role because he knows what it is like to have nothing. Sold to Egypt as a slave,[11] then falsely accused of rape and thrown into prison,[12] it wasn't until he was asked to interpret the king of Egypt's dreams that his circumstances dramatically improved. Thanks to his revelation that fat cows represented an abundant feast of food, the prisoner was awarded a position of respect, the king's own royal ring, and *fine linen clothes*.[13]

In the midst of a pirouette, the storyteller in Elohim continues with a tale of a poverty-stricken son returning home. '"*Hurry!*" the father shouts. "*Bring the best clothes and put them on* my son. *Put a ring on his finger... get a fat calf and kill it so we can have a feast and celebrate. My son was dead, but now he is alive.*"'[14]

As Jacob's sons reach the front of the queue and bow before the governor,[15] Elohim edges further forward, animated by the prospect of another extraordinary family reunion.

For this governor is Joseph - Jacob's Joseph.

Out of the blue, the firstborn of Rachel has been presented with a remarkable opportunity. Because the lost son wants nothing more than to rest once again in his father's arms. And to hear him celebrate, '*My son was dead, but now he is alive.*'

1. Genesis 33:4
2. Genesis 33:10
3. Luke 15:20 (NIV)
4. Genesis 29:17
5. Genesis 29:20
6. Genesis 30:7-20
7. Genesis 30:22-24
8. Genesis 35:16-18
9. Genesis 37:33
10. Genesis 42:1-2
11. Genesis 37:28
12. Genesis 39:20
13. Genesis 41:42
14. Luke 15:22-24
15. Genesis 42:6

2.05 – They Face Execution

Despite the most unquenchable desire to see his father, the sight of his ten brothers causes every emotion of Joseph to be hijacked by anger. It's like his eyes catch fire as fury explodes. *'You are spies!'*[1] Joseph bellows, pointing his finger furiously.

A deathly silence falls. All in the bustling marketplace are stunned. Shivers shoot down the brothers' spines as their frantic protests fall on deaf ears and the ten are dragged away under arrest, bewildered and aghast, oblivious to the proximity of their long-lost sibling.

Joseph sits paralysed, locked in rage, poised to lash out like a wounded animal. With every eye on him, the governor simply wishes the ground would swallow him up. He bites his lip, desperate to maintain dignity. Inside, the throbbing pains of age-old scars pulse through every fibre of his being as his mind replays the events which cut his wounds raw: the day he was stripped naked, dragged across dirt, hurled down a well and traded into slavery.[2]

By his own brothers.

His own jealousy-fuelled brothers.

Embarrassed, Joseph rises to his feet and walks sheepishly through the speechless crowds.

Stripped.

Dragged.

Hurled.

Traded.

Deeply suppressed bitterness and fear is excavated as the memories play over and over. But another image niggles away, that of his aging father desperate for food. Torn to the core, Joseph wrestles a longing to rescue against a lust for revenge. Pulled apart by hatred and love, eventually he settles upon a compromise.

'If you are honest men,' the governor tells his captives, *'let one of your brothers stay here in prison while the rest of you go and carry grain back to your hungry families. Then bring your youngest brother back here to me. If you do this… you will not die.'*[3]

Repulsed by the ultimatum, Jacob rocks his head back then clenches his eyes. *'Everything is against me,'*[4] he sighs at his sons. *'I will not allow Benjamin to go with you. He is the only son left from my wife Rachel. If anything happened to him… I would be sad until the day I die.'*[5]

Joseph's brothers feel hopelessly trapped. With their grain sacks already empty, they must return to Egypt to survive. Yet without Benjamin, they face execution.

Shaken by his father's distress, Judah falls to his knees and takes hold of Jacob's dry, wrinkled hand. *'Send Benjamin with me,'* he begs. *'I will guarantee you his safety, and I will be personally responsible for him.'*[6]

Their eyes locked, Judah sees far into his father's agony.

Head in hands and shoulders slumped, Jacob slowly

nods. As the frail father sits pale faced, drawn and motionless, seemingly stripped of all emotion, he hardly notices his sons' tender kisses goodbye. All afternoon and evening, Jacob stares straight-ahead, eyes fixed on the point where Benjamin disappeared from sight. Alone, with no energy to move, only now do tears drip from his chin one by one.

Why, God, why?

Why be so cruel?

Cutting the back of his throat, an infuriated cry slices the cool night sky.

Once more, Joseph's brothers are before him.

Once again, they are wrongfully under arrest.

Only this time, the prosecution has plenty of evidence.

Benjamin has been caught red-handed.

Stealing a precious royal cup.

Yet Benjamin is entirely innocent. Joseph has meticulously manufactured the scenario so that Rachel's second son shares the same fate as her first: unjust imprisonment and slavery.

As powerful as the king[7] - able to dispense his revenge in an instant - the governor watches his brothers closely. Have they changed? Or are they as selfish as ever; cold, callous and cowardly?

Judah steps forward, his vow to protect Benjamin swirling in his stomach. *'Master, what can we say? How can we show we are not guilty?'*[8]

Joseph sidesteps the question: *'The man who stole the cup will be my slave. The rest of you may go back safely to your father.'*[9]

Picturing his father's agony, seeing Jacob's unending misery, Judah clutches his chest and rips his clothes. *'Please allow me to stay here and be your slave. Let the young boy go back home with his brothers. I cannot go back to my father if the boy is not with me. I cannot stand to see my father that sad.'*[10]

Joseph stares transfixed, not quite believing his eyes; Judah is a man totally transformed from the brother he once knew.

Sacrifice has replaced selfishness.

Empathy has replaced jealousy.

Compassion has replaced hatred.

Unable to control himself any longer, the respected ruler breaks down, weeping inconsolably, releasing over a decade of pent up emotion.

'I am...'

Brushing away tears, Joseph looks up into his brothers' frightened eyes.

'I am Joseph. Is my father still alive?'[11]

A great liberated smile fills Judah's cheeks as he watches Joseph and Benjamin embrace. Previously, Judah would have hated this sight: the favourite sons of Jacob - the two golden boys - together again.

But today... today, Judah was the reason for this reunion; he was the catalyst.

And not since childhood has joy felt like this.

The Community of Elohim beams with colossal paternal pride; in their Rescue Mission, progress is made when individuals offer themselves in place of others.

1.   Genesis 42:9
2.   Genesis 37:23-28
3.   Genesis 42:20
4.   Genesis 42:36
5.   Genesis 42:38
6.   Genesis 43:8-9
7.   Genesis 44:18
8.   Genesis 44:16
9.   Genesis 44:17
10. Genesis 44:33-34
11. Genesis 45:3

2.06 – Return Home

'Joseph is alive.'

Lost in heavy slumber, Jacob groans.

'Joseph is alive.'

Jacob's head rocks chaotically, as if tortured by a dream.

'Joseph is alive.'

The voice is getting louder, clearer. And somewhere in the sleeper's consciousness he registers hands holding - shaking - his shoulders. Slowly, Jacob opens his eyes. There before him is Benjamin, grinning wildly.

'Joseph is alive.'

One after another Jacob's sons squeeze their father's fragile frame. Through the glorious hubbub, the warmth of each hug rouses Jacob's senses, waking him fully to the world. In the embrace of Simeon, free from Egyptian prison, estranged remnants of joy return home to his heart; Jacob even manages a laugh. And it is here, wrapped within the arms of his lost son, that the words finally strike home: Joseph is alive!

Urgently, desperately, Jacob looks around.

One, two, three... ten, eleven.

'Joseph is alive,' Benjamin repeats again, eyes resonating with conviction. His father looks around again, not knowing what to think. Each son fidgets with genuine excitement; perhaps it is true. Jacob chooses to take hold of a fragment of hope.

'*Joseph is still alive,*' says Judah, jumping on the spot, 'and he is *ruler over all the land of Egypt.*'[1]

Jacob's heart sinks like a rock. His eyes roll, turning to the heavens in disgust. My own sons, why do they lie? Joseph: ruler in Egypt? Why be so far-fetched?

Benjamin takes his father gently by the hand.

'Let me show you something.'

Reluctantly, Jacob nods.

He follows Benjamin outside.

Where he finds several majestic wooden wagons.

The finest Egyptian wooden wagons.

'The king of Egypt gave these to us.'[2]

Jacob stands rigid, not knowing whether to laugh or cry. Over the passing minutes he becomes increasingly mesmerised. A warm gush of love flows through his stomach, dissipating all aggravated tension; and before long, it's as if he is standing alone with Joseph. Moving with ease, Jacob draws beside the vehicles and places his palm on the wood.

Tenderly, he strokes.

'*Now I believe you.*[3] Gather everything; we are moving to Egypt!'

Overjoyed by the spectacle, in the Community of Elohim the Father reaches for his Son's hands, opens up the palms, and tenderly strokes his Son's wrists. Their faces exude absolute, united determination.

Their Rescue Mission is underway.

They have laid the foundations.

Thanks to Joseph's lifesaving accomplishments,

Elohim's chosen children have survived imminent starvation and are now enjoying the finest luxuries[4] and *the best land in Egypt*.[5] But what most thrills Father and Son is Joseph's growing awareness of their involvement in events: *'Don't be worried or angry with yourselves because you sold me here,'* Joseph told his brothers, *'God sent me here ahead of you to save people's lives.'*[6]

Anticipating the events about to unfold, Father and Son fling arms around each other and together as one they savour the spectacular sight of Joseph rushing into the outstretched arms of his long-lost father. And when Joseph turns to his brothers with forgiveness shimmering in his eyes and announces, *'God turned your evil into good,'*[7] euphoria reigns and hope soars in the electrifying Elohim.

Because together, this community is Love.

And Love is transformation.

Love is turning filth into beauty.

Love is making all things new.

And at last, those who are loved so dearly are beginning to recognise Love's revolutionary potential; Love's revolutionary power.

Next on the wall, we learn that Jacob's name has changed to 'Israel'.[8] Intrigued, we step back to survey the entire Phase One and Phase Two wall, searching for a significance to this switch.

The first thing that strikes us is how cluttered and untidy everything appears. Across every generation, deceit and betrayal have ripped relationships apart.

Yet, by drawing alongside individuals, the Rescue Strategists have successfully encouraged honesty and loyalty to triumph; and in the process, their rescue ambitions have progressed.

But Egypt, we remember, is not the land promised to Abraham. That land is still inhabited by the descendants Noah cursed: the Canaanites.

We turn through ninety degrees to face the wall adjacent. Suddenly, we see it: beneath a striking 'Phase Three' heading, painted in the middle of a giant map, here is a nation called 'Israel'.

The land of Israel is divided into twelve regions.

One is labelled, 'Judah.'

Another is 'Benjamin.'

The regions, we quickly deduce, are named after Jacob's twelve sons.

Satisfied, we turn back to read the conclusion to Phase Two.

'*I am about to die,*' Joseph tells his brothers. His frail voice contains no sorrow; just optimism and assurance. '*God will take care of you. He will lead you out of this land to the land he promised to Abraham, Isaac and Jacob.*'[9]

Reaching for breath, Joseph gasps, '*Promise me that you will carry my bones with you out of Egypt.*'[10] Then the saviour of Egypt closes his eyes and lets go of his life.

Joseph's body is mummified and laid to rest.

In a coffin.

In Egypt.[11]

Ever since arriving in Egypt as a slave, Joseph never once returned to Canaan; he never once returned home.

Over four hundred years will pass before Joseph gets his dying wish. Not until the conclusion to Phase Three will Joseph finally return home.[12]

1. Genesis 45:26
2. Genesis 45:27
3. Genesis 45:28
4. Genesis 45:20
5. Genesis 45:18
6. Genesis 45:5
7. Genesis 50:20
8. Genesis 32:28
9. Genesis 50:24
10. Genesis 50:25
11. Genesis 50:26
12. Joshua 24:3

PHASE THREE

3.01 – I Called My Son

Responding to agonised cries, three friends traipse across arid desert. Pyramids may decorate the horizon but this group walks with heads bowed to the dusty ground. They are driven onwards by an epic united ambition. Together, they cross the barren wilderness in search of one man to end oppression, one man to end suffering, one man to rescue.

In unison all three draw to a halt. The Father of the group reaches out his hand, and wipes away teardrops swept chaotically across his Son's face. 'We must keep going,' he whispers slowly.

Over the past four hundred years, the Community of Elohim has experienced increasing isolation, betrayal and pain. Egypt was only ever intended as a temporary home, precious respite en-route to a far greater destination. With the food crisis long over, the Israelites could have left Egypt in pursuit of their own promised, covenanted land.

But God's promises were ignored.

The Israelites remained in Egypt.

And covenant progress stalled.

Born to promote the Creator's character, Abraham's descendants need to grow and mature in close relationship with their Father. But as generations passed, far from developing differences, the Israelites embedded further into the fabric of Egyptian society.

Adopting their culture.

Adopting their ideals.

Adopting their gods.

'Your descendants will be strangers and travel in a land they don't own,' Elohim once warned Abram in a dark, terrifying nightmare, *'The people there will make them slaves.'*[1] And sure enough, when *a new king began to rule Egypt, who did not know who Joseph was,*[2] he wasted no time in putting the Israelites to work on ambitious construction projects.

The slave drivers showed no mercy, demanding more and more.

Thrashing.

Beating.

Whipping them into action.

For over a century, the three desert explorers have flinched as leather slices Israelite skin, with ever increasing intensity. Oppression eventually escalated to sadistic proportions when - fearing an uprising - the new Pharaoh decreed, *'Every time a boy is born to the* Israelites, *you must throw him into the Nile River.'*[3]

Mourning the innocent screams of their drowning infants, Elohim's agony stokes furious flames of anger.

'Moses, Moses!'[4]

A nearby shepherd staggers back, cowering in fright.

The bush before him is on fire but not burning up.

'Do not come any closer. Take off your sandals, because you

are standing on holy ground. I am the God of your ancestors - the God of Abraham, the God of Isaac and the God of Jacob.'[5]

Anticipating thunderous judgement, Moses covers his eyes. His chest contracts so tightly his whole body quivers.

'I have seen the troubles my people have suffered, and I have heard their cries.'[6]

The raw emotion catches Moses by surprise.

Not just heartfelt, this voice is heartbroken.

'So now I am sending you to the king of Egypt. Go! Bring my people, the Israelites, out of Egypt!'[7]

Moses' hands slide slowly down his face.

As the statement sinks in, one bewildering question thumps within.

How?

How?

How can I go to the King?[8]

After all, Moses is a wanted man.

Wanted for murder.

Indeed, when Moses struck down a slave driver and buried his body in the sand,[9] the Community of Elohim found their man; here was an Israelite who shared their burning rage in the face of injustice and suffering.

As Moses' question stutters and stumbles out, Love's response is instant: *'I will be with you.'*[10]

'But what if the people ask for your name? *What should I tell them?'*

'Tell them I AM WHO I AM *sent me to you.'*[11]

Or equally, I WILL BE WHO I WILL BE.

Each meaning is encapsulated by 'Yahweh'.

Unlike 'Elohim', which refers to an all-powerful Creator, 'Yahweh' is a personal, relational name.

An intimate name.

A mysterious, indefinable, all-encompassing name.

'This will always be my name,' explains Yahweh, *'by which people from now on will know me.'*[12]

Interrupting the narrative, a note covers the next portion of text. Taped across its top edge, the supplementary flap switches the scene:

Escaping an imminent slaughter of infants, a young couple flee with babe in arms, knowing that their nation's entire hopes of liberation rest on their young boy's survival. Taking refuge in Egypt, Mary and Joseph remain in hiding until all those trying to kill their firstborn son have died.[13]

Concluding the additional account, we read, *'All this happened to bring about what* Yahweh *said through the prophet: "I called my son out of Egypt."'*[14]

We double take.

Does this really mean…?

Could a human child really be Yahweh's son?

Already intrigued by repeating themes of 'liberation' and 'out of Egypt', an arrow informs us that three-month-old Moses was also saved from massacre by the quick thinking of his mother. Placed in a basket

- covered in tar *so that it would float*[15] - young Moses sailed down the Nile, no doubt passing countless innocent corpses in the depths below.

Underneath the flap, the Moses narrative continues.

And so do the parallels.

'The men who wanted to kill you are dead,'[16] Yahweh tells Moses. 'Now return to Egypt and proclaim on my behalf: *'Israel is my firstborn son.'*[17]

1. Genesis 15:13
2. Exodus 1:8
3. Exodus 1:22
4. Exodus 3:4
5. Exodus 3:5-6
6. Exodus 3:7
7. Exodus 3:10
8. Exodus 3:11
9. Exodus 2:11-12
10. Exodus 3:12
11. Exodus 3:13-14
12. Exodus 3:15
13. Matthew 2:20
14. Matthew 2:15
15. Exodus 2:3
16. Exodus 4:19
17. Exodus 4:22

3.02 – And Kiss

Absorbing the Israelites' fury, Moses pounds a pile of pyramid bricks then slumps down within a sloppy mixture of straw and clay. *'Why have you brought this trouble on your people?'* he cries, deflecting his incandescent rage skywards. *'You have done nothing to save them.'*[1]

Abandoned.

Alone.

Betrayed.

Moses' uprising has been a laughing stock.

He has merely made the Israelites' suffering worse.[2]

'Who is Yahweh?*'* Pharaoh had simply sneered, aggravated by the sheer arrogance and ambiguity of the name. *'Why should I obey him and let Israel go? I do not know Yahweh.'*[3]

Moses should have seen it coming. No credible power would align itself with slaves. The gods favour Pharaoh; for indeed, Pharaoh is a god.

Declaring war on Egypt's invented imitation gods, Yahweh's roar reverberates through Moses' bones. *'I will punish Egypt with my power, and I will bring the Israelites out of that land. Then they will know that I am* Yahweh.*'*[4] And at the resting place of the Israelites' murdered infants, retribution begins.

The River Nile turns to blood, killing all aquatic life.[5]
Striking at the moment of the Nile god Hapi's greatest yearly achievement, when the banks overflow and fertilise the land, this year's flooding will contaminate all crops; and thoroughly humiliate Hapi.

Up from the river bound multitudes of frogs.[6]
Multiplying annually after the flooding, frogs are a symbol of prosperity in Egypt. Even the goddess Heqet takes the form of a frog. But the extremity of this year's population surge turns Heqet into a nauseating nuisance, an absolute pest.

Drawn to the repulsive aura, gnats throng the air.[7]
So far, Pharaoh's magicians have managed to imitate both the blood and frogs phenomena, undermining Yahweh's credibility. This time, however, they have no such success, forcing the sorcerers to acknowledge their nemesis' superiority.[8]

In the gnats' wake, swarms of flies descend.[9]
'I will not treat the Israelites the same as the Egyptians,'[10] Yahweh promised. And sure enough, to the Egyptians' horror and utter disbelief, every Israelite home escapes infestation. No longer in the realms of sorcery, this is miraculous.

Overnight, all Egyptian livestock is decimated.
Integral to Egypt's economic prosperity, many of the nation's gods - such as Hathor and Apis - take the

appearance of cattle. But in one fell swoop Yahweh undeniably humiliates these powers. And once again, the Israelites are left unscathed.[11]

Across human skin, boils throb furiously.[12]

'Stop!' we shout. 'Enough!'
Our knees trembling, we look on in dismay.
This is annihilation. This is torture.

Accused of callous cruelty, Love counters: this is restrained.
'By now,' Yahweh informs Pharaoh, *'I could have... caused a terrible disease that would have destroyed you and your people from the earth. But I have let you live for this reason... so that my name will be talked about in all the earth.'*[13]

Accompanied by lightning, a thunderous hail storm erupts.[14]
'Let the Israelites go,' the King's advisers beg, desperate for some respite. *'Don't you know that Egypt is ruined?'*[15]
Yet from the sanctuary of his throne, the King remains unmoved, unaffected, untouched by the terrors.

A plague of locusts strips all vegetation bare.[16]
Sounding the death knell for Egypt's economy, at last Pharaoh is concerned. But letting his slaves go would be foolish: it will only make them stronger; and the Israelites represent some of Egypt's only remaining

wealth.

Three days of darkness engulfs the land.[17]
Only now does Pharaoh concede his gods have lost. Even the mighty powers of Ra, controller of the sun, have been eclipsed. Indeed, the only Egyptian gods who remain undefeated are Pharaoh himself and Pharaoh's firstborn son.

'I will punish all the gods of Egypt.[18] *About midnight tonight,'* Yahweh tells Moses, *'every firstborn son... will die.*[19] But smear onto your doorframes the blood of a lamb - *a one-year-old male that has nothing wrong with it*[20] - and *when I see the blood, I will pass over you.'*[21]

Hearing Egypt's excruciating cries of grief our knees give way as we crash to the ground.
How is this love?
How is this fair?
In the cold light of day, setting emotions aside, perhaps we could just about rationalise that - after Egypt's unremorseful drowning of Yahweh's own babies - this is justice; this is proportionate, reciprocated revenge.
But what we are really struggling to understand is why - after mocking, scorning and resenting Yahweh's affection - why should the Israelites receive such favour; such disproportionate, undeserved grace?
It's suffering for one and ecstasy for the other.
Justice and Grace, how can both be of God?
How can both find their home in Love?

They seem so contradictory.
So incompatible.

Tonight, as thousands lose their lives, yet thousands are spared, a prototype is presented. The Israelites' exclusive rescue is a foretaste of a future limitless redemption where Love sees the blood of an innocent lamb and judgement and death pass over all nationalities. On that day, Justice and Grace will hold hands, look each other in the eye, and kiss.[22]

1. Exodus 5:21-23
2. Exodus 5:9
3. Exodus 5:2
4. Exodus 7:5
5. Exodus 7:20
6. Exodus 8:6
7. Exodus 8:17
8. Exodus 8:18-19
9. Exodus 8:24
10. Exodus 8:22
11. Exodus 9:6
12. Exodus 9:10
13. Exodus 9:15-16
14. Exodus 9:23
15. Exodus 10:7
16. Exodus 10:14
17. Exodus 10:22
18. Exodus 12:12
19. Exodus 11:4-5
20. Exodus 12:5
21. Exodus 12:13
22. Romans 3:24-25

3.03 – From Death Comes Life

Cheers of euphoria are joined by the roar of pounding feet as the sight of a vast sea of bodies, hundreds of thousands, perhaps millions strong, floods Moses with immense pride. Gone are his hesitant nerves; this is the impossible dream, reality before his very eyes.

'Get out! *Leave my people,*' the King had howled, bent over his son's cold, limp body, *'go and worship* Yahweh.'[1]

Moses left the palace unable to stifle a smile.

Because out from death comes life for his people.

'*Remember this day,*'[2] Moses cries out to the masses.

From now on, every event must be viewed in light of today. *This month will be the beginning of months;*[3] a new era has begun.

Equally, their future freedom builds upon past foundations. And by holding the mummified body of their great ancestor Joseph, Moses communicates this message in the most vivid way possible. '*When God saves you,*' Joseph had asserted confidently, '*remember to carry my bones with you out of Egypt.*'[4]

Moses is fulfilling Joseph's dying wish.

Still knelt by his son, the raucous sound of mass exodus, deafening like the crashing of waves, further ignites Pharaoh's rage. The King rises to his feet and watches from his window as wave after wave cross his nation's border.

Then it dawns.

The crowds carry with them every possible possession. They have no intention of returning after worshipping Yahweh.

His eyes a furious bloodshot red, Pharaoh flings his fist into the wall. *'What have we done?'* he screeches. *'We have lost our slaves!*[5] Stop them!'

Used to a diet of deities that the Israelites' can see and touch, Yahweh leaves his children in no doubt of his presence with them, leading the way southeastward by a remarkable, unmissable pillar of cloud.

The challenge of moving such substantial numbers, together with the scorching heat, makes progress slow. Reaching a large stretch of water, a rarity in the deserts beyond, Moses opts to make camp as evening draws in.

Exhausted, many take the opportunity to wash in the refreshing waters. Mothers watch their children closely, careful not to let them venture in too deep, beyond where reeds protrude the surface.

For a while laughter fills the air.

Before all of a sudden, the water starts to ripple, as if shaking angrily.

All turn to face the desert. Far off, a mighty sandstorm approaches, accompanied by an ominously familiar rumbling sound. Swinging their heads back and forth, from desert to sea, a terrifying realisation sets in: this is the storm of Egyptian chariots charging at full pelt; and there is no escape.

'*What have you done to us*, Moses?'[6]

'We told you to leave us alone!'

'We are going to die in this desert!'[7]

'*Don't be afraid!*' Moses roars, bringing an unerring hush to the commotion. '*Stand still and you will see* Yahweh *save you today.*'[8]

Immediately, Yahweh's swirling cloud intercepts the course of the galloping horses, causing the horses to bolt, frightened by the fog. Bringing the chaos under control, the Egyptian generals halt their pursuit. The Israelites are trapped; there is no need to take unnecessary risks.

Next, Moses - perfectly following orders[9] - stretches his hand out over the waters.

Rushing eastward a gale blows in.

Colliding.

Driving.

Lashing back the waters.

Exposing the bed of reeds.

All night, faces etched with awe and wonder cross the partitioned seas, churning up the sodden surface. On the other side of the water, shocked chariot drivers crack their whips, urging their horses forward in quick pursuit. Wheels toss mud high into the air, hooves sink into the quagmire, stallions buckle and crash; and reputable army generals fling themselves to the ground, shrieking '*Let's get away from the Israelites!* Yahweh *is fighting for them and against Egypt.*'[10]

As the sun rises on a brand new day, the storming winds cease.

Sending waves crashing down.

Some die on impact.

The rest flail in the depths until they can breathe no more.

Overcome with sorrow, yet overflowing with joy, the lovers of Elohim look forward, longing and waiting, aching in anticipation for the day when the whole of creation is brought out from slavery into *glorious freedom.*[11]

Wave after wave of wonderful singing washes over the trio as Abraham's descendants - caked in dirt and dancing with delight - burst into spontaneous song:

'Are there any gods like you, Yahweh?

There are no gods like you.

You are wonderfully holy,

amazingly powerful,

a worker of miracles.

You reached out your right hand

and the earth swallowed our enemies.'[12]

Encouraged by new levels of understanding, trust and respect, one friend reaches down and energetically sketches a picture of fishing vessels caught in a torrential storm. In the artist's image, one man stands unperturbed on the prow of his boat, winds and waves pelting his frame.

'Quiet! Be still,'[13] says the illustrator.

In the picture, the waters calm, cowering in retreat.

'Who is this?' one friend asks with a knowing, playful grin, pointing at the man in the artwork. *'Even the*

winds and waves obey him!'[14]
Laughing, two friends lovingly wrap arms around the third.
'This is my Son, whom I love; with him I am well pleased.'[15]

1. Exodus 12:31
2. Exodus 13:3
3. Exodus 12:2
4. Exodus 13:19
5. Exodus 14:5
6. Exodus 14:11
7. Exodus 14:12
8. Exodus 14:13
9. Exodus 14:16
10. Exodus 14:25
11. Romans 8:21
12. Exodus 15:11
13. Mark 4:39
14. Mark 4:41
15. Matthew 3:17 (NIV)

3.04 – The Proposal

Across a solid blue backdrop rich golden rays fill the sky. Energetic beams bounce off the sands causing a dazzling sparkle all around. Exposed to the sun, the desert floor burns scorching hot.

And on sore, blistered, throbbing feet, hundreds of thousands of Israelites trudge.

Trudge.

Trudge.

Trudge.

Every man, woman and child drips with sweat, desperate for shade.

'What kind of freedom is this?' the first mutters arise.

'This is more like torture.'

'*Is* Yahweh *with us or not?*'[1]

'At least in Egypt we ate *cucumbers, melons, leeks, onions and garlic.*'[2]

'*It would have been better if* Yahweh *had killed us in Egypt.*'[3]

We jolt. After everything...

How could they be so impatient?

So insensitive?

So insulting?

Responding to the cries of the liberated, small white seeds - tasting *like wafers made from honey*[4] - drop daily from the sky. A double helping falls every sixth day, enabling every seventh day to be set aside as a Sabbath, a *day of rest*;[5] a day to appreciate, contemplate and celebrate freedom from the unending daily cycle of relentless, back-breaking labour.

Yahweh's instruction is simple.

Do not search for food on a Sabbath.

The sun rises on the inaugural day of rest.

And several Israelites set out in search of food.[6]

In the midst of our bewilderment, we take a step back.

This is exasperating.

Yet not entirely surprising.

Having spent their entire lives embedded in Egyptian culture, surrounded by a multitude of gods, with no cultural identity of their own, it is not going to be easy for the Israelites to change their ways, to change the habits of a lifetime.

Removing the Israelites from Egypt was one thing.

Removing Egypt from the Israelites is another.

'How long will you refuse to obey my commands and teachings?'[7] the embracing Elohim sighs poignantly as the trio arch forward in anticipation, poised to unveil, not just one, but hundreds of new instructions for living in a highly significant new covenant.

Until now, Love's covenants have, in the most part, been unconditional; they have been incessant and generous one-way displays of affection, regardless of response.

But Love desires response.

Partnership.

Collaboration.

Commitment.

This time the contract will be proposed before it is signed.

Second class citizens their entire lives, the liberated slaves will be invited to play their part in the liberation of the entire world.

If chosen, the Israelites will stand out as an advert for the Creator's character.

If chosen, all nations will be attracted towards an alternative, healthier lifestyle.

If chosen, creation will take a giant leap towards its originally intended paradise.

No more murder.

No more adultery.

No more robbery.

No more deception.

No more jealousy.[8]

'This will be the proof that I am sending you', Elohim announced on the day Moses' life transformed from obscurity to prominence. *'After you lead the people out of Egypt, all of you will worship me on this mountain.'*[9]

And *exactly three months after* leaving *Egypt*,[10] Moses reaches out and caresses the colossus Mount Sinai, grinning wide with wonder, satisfied and besotted, revelling in this unshakable proof of Yahweh's unfathomable affection.

'Every one of you', Love's proposal begins, 'has seen *how*

I carried you out of Egypt as if on eagle's wings...'

I choose you.
I care for you.
I love you.

'...And I brought you here to me.'[11]

I want relationship with you.

'If you obey me and keep my agreement, you will be my own possession, chosen from all nations.'[12]

The Lover gets down on one knee.

'You must not have any other gods except me.[13]
'You must not use gold or silver to make idols.'[14]

Will you choose me?
Will you love me?
Forsaking all others, will you marry me?

Apprehension rises in our gut.
This is a proposal of permanent, exclusive, mutual love. Yet the Israelites' affections appear shallow and fickle, far from consistent.
This is a risk.

Thick, dramatic cloud covers the mountain.
Thunder and lightning roar.

Everyone trembles.
And the Lover's heart skips a beat, awaiting response.

Yes, we choose you.
Yes, we will marry you.
We will do everything that you have *said*.[15]

Climbing high into Sinai, Moses' heart pounds as he is ushered inside Elohim's embrace; and in a spectacular celebration of intimacy, he sees the God of Israel standing on a blue sapphire surface as *clear as the sky itself*.[16] Delighting in Moses' company, the newly engaged lovers seal their covenant commitment with a feast;[17] before Love cheers with absolute, abounding joy, *'I will live with the people of Israel and be their God.'*[18]

Below the mountain, a golden calf is constructed, similar in appearance to the Egyptian goddess Hathor. *'Israel,'* it is announced, *'these are your gods who brought you out of the land of Egypt.'*[19]

1. Exodus 17:7
2. Numbers 11:5
3. Exodus 16:3
4. Exodus 16:31
5. Exodus 16:25
6. Exodus 16:27
7. Exodus 16:28
8. Exodus 19:1
9. Exodus 20:13–17
10. Exodus 3:12
11. Exodus 19:4
12. Exodus 19:5
13. Exodus 20:3
14. Exodus 20:23
15. Exodus 19:8
16. Exodus 24:10
17. Exodus 24:11
18. Exodus 29:45
19. Exodus 32:4

3.05 – You Shall Save Three Thousand

Dead bodies lie scattered across blood-soaked ground. A chilling silence fills the air; a silence completely contrasting recent celebrations of a golden calf, a silence pierced only by sporadic grief-stricken howls.

Moses buckles over, sickened by the sight, nauseated by the stench, vomiting in the knowledge that he himself instigated these deaths; he gave the order for this purge of three thousand Israelites.

But what else could he have done?

He had shown Yahweh's fury.

He had smashed the tablets of the law.[1]

He had stressed the severity, conveyed the gravity.

He had spurned an opportunity to become like Abraham.

He had stopped wholesale Noah-like destruction.

He had changed Yahweh's mind.[2]

Yet when he offered the Israelites redemption, declaring, *'Let anyone who wants to follow* Yahweh *come to me,'*[3] to Moses' sheer gut-wrenching horror, only the family of Levi stepped forward to receive his reprieve.

The Levites chose life.

The rest chose death.[4]

Tears trace through the dirt and dust smeared cheeks of all those shaking in terror. In their haunted, petrified eyes, Moses sees a deep, tortured regret: at last, all have grasped the significance of keeping the law.

Yahweh was not exaggerating: death really is the consequence of disobedience.

And so too is separation.

Disconnection from their Lover.

Their Liberator.

Their Protector.

Their Guide.

'I will not go with you', Yahweh announced, *'because I might destroy you on the way.'*[5]

'But, but…'

Whether God is listening or not we want to shout out in protest. But we do not dare. Fear holds our mouth shut.

We want to tell God that in many ways we understand. We get that Love requires justice. We get that broken laws must carry consequences. And we get that punishments will deter future anarchy. We get all that. But… but… isn't this meant to be a Rescue Mission? At the moment, this is just slaughter.

In the midst of our bewilderment, a dramatic poster catches our eye.

On the left, vibrantly coloured: peace, protection, prosperity.[6]

On the right, in a dark, constrictive web: disease, starvation, destruction.[7]

And in the centre, in elegant, vivid white, we read: *'If these disobedient people are sorry… and accept punishment for their sin, I will remember my agreement,*[8] and I will not *completely destroy them.'*[9]

Sin: the word appears to encapsulate every kind of disobedience, every boundary broken.

Sin is what corrupts beauty.

Sin is what causes division.

Sin is what deserves punishment.

Yet remorse over sin ensures continuation.

Remorse averts complete annihilation.

But that is all; there is no progress here; no life, no liberation. God, we would urge, if we dared shout out, you need to find some other way to deal with sin.

United in grief, mourning the loss of three thousand dearly-loved lives, three friends find comfort in each other's tender affection. The Community of Elohim grip each other tightly, desperate to contain all their devastated anger within their embrace.

The trio may have had to withdraw from relationship, but pure, pulsating, mesmerised Love is unable to avert its gaze. They watch intently, intrigued and enthralled, as Moses sets about constructing an elegant linen tent with *blue, purple and red thread*.[10]

'Look how much Moses wants us,' Abba beams. 'Moses still believes intimacy is possible.'

'Drenched by his tears, Moses bowed low before us and offered himself in place of those that deserved punishment.[11] Moses connected with the heart of our liberation plan. The blood of an animal shall be shed as a substitute, a proxy. This is justice and grace holding hands, giving our children a chance to start again in pursuit of beauty.'

'Then we can live together,' adds the third friend excitedly.

'Oh, Ruach, you shall dwell within a glorious room inside Moses tent.[12] They will call it the 'Holy of Holies,' because you are so stunningly beautiful.'

'I cannot wait,' says Ruach, her eyes shining with delight. 'Then only the thickness of a curtain will separate us from humans.'

'Once a year, one man shall step beyond the curtain into your Holy of Holies.[13] Before entering, the anointed Levite will hold a living goat and confess over it *all the sins and crimes of Israel… Then he will send the goat away into the desert.*'[14]

'Yes! That way our loved ones will see their sins running away from them, never to return again. The sight should convince them that their sins really are no more; that they really are forgiven, free and clean.'

'Abba, let's replace the stone slabs which Moses smashed,[15] and place the laws inside the Holy of Holies. And let's establish a festival to ensure no-one ever forgets these events at Sinai. Every year, *on the day of firstfruits,*[16] celebrating a bountiful harvest, our children shall reflect upon the beginnings of our relationship, and remember the tragic loss of three thousand. Taking place fifty days after Passover, the event will become known as Pentecost.'

'And at one future Pentecost, Ruach, after the world-changing events of that year's Passover, you shall save three thousand lives.'[17]

Ruach bristles with elation. She wraps around Father

and Son, enveloping them in ultimate joy. 'I will put the law *in their minds and write it on their hearts.*'[18]

'Come, my love, let's speak to Moses *face to face as a man speaks with a friend.*'[19]

'Oh, how his face shall shine,'[20] Ruach replies, grinning wildly.

'Come, let's fill Moses' marvellous tent.'

'Let's go travelling with our fiancé.'

1.   Exodus 32:19
2.   Exodus 32:10–14
3.   Exodus 32:26
4.   Exodus 32:27
5.   Exodus 33:3
6.   Leviticus 26:5–6
7.   Leviticus 26:16
8.   Leviticus 26:41–42
9.   Leviticus 26:45
10. Exodus 26:1
11. Exodus 32:32
12. Leviticus 26:11–12
13. Leviticus 16:2–3
14. Leviticus 16:21
15. Exodus 34:1
16. Numbers 28:26
17. Acts 2:41
18. Jeremiah 31:33 (NIV)
19. Exodus 33:11
20. Exodus 34:29

3.06 – The Splattered Mess

Head resting on his elbow, Joshua lies with eyes affectionately fixed upon Yahweh's ferocious flames. Where once mysterious, far-off powers could only be revered in the form of lifeless carvings - rigid and static - this god Yahweh draws close, swirling and flickering with wild animation. Fire by night, cloud by day, this god who steals the heart watches and protects with unprecedented intimacy.

For the last eleven days, Yahweh's dynamic pillar of cloud[1] has steered the Israelites north from Sinai with authority, patience and provision. Traversing hot and hostile deserts, their route took in a long refreshing coastline, rich in nutritious quail.[2]

Now the Israelites camp on the brink of a lush and fertile land.

Not that Joshua has ever seen the land, of course; no-one has. The only paradise the Israelites have ever glimpsed was in the north-east of Egypt: a sumptuous land of flowing rivers and thriving greenery. But that was a relatively small region. To the Israelites, the rest of the world is merely an endless vista of golden sands, the occasional oasis of water and clusters of jagged mountains.

Rather curiously, all Joshua knows for sure about the Promised Land is that it was cursed long ago by Noah.[3] Indeed, the last time Canaan was home to

Abraham's descendants, it was gripped by crippling drought.[4] Yet Joshua sees no reason to doubt Yahweh's promise now; if this god can liberate slaves, then he can surely overhaul a desolate curse.

On exiting Egypt, Joshua's amateur army secured a surprise victory over the Amalekites.[5] Strong and disciplined, the former slaves possessed raw potential. Now, more than a year later, they are a respectable fighting force: trained, drilled and tactically united, with all tribes marching in a strict regimented formation, encircling Yahweh's resplendent tabernacle. Like a child on the eve of a great celebration, Joshua grins.

He can sense it in his gut.

Today is the day.

'Are there any gods like you, Lord?' his heart sings. *'You are wonderfully holy, amazingly powerful, a worker of miracles.'*[6] Lost in adulation, Moses' liberation lyrics continue to race without restraint, passing the hours until bright shining light emerges from the east and Moses' familiar trumpet call welcomes the dawn.

Greeting the day Joshua has been waiting for his entire life; the day the Israelites reach the Promised Land.

Under a rich blue sky, Joshua climbs to the peak of Canaan's mountainous border. Standing with arms outstretched, wind blowing through his hair, Joshua feels light enough to fly; indeed his heart is soaring. He is looking out at a panorama of paradise, an unending ocean of greenery.

'You keep your loving promise and lead the people you have saved,' Joshua cries at the top of his lungs. *'With your strength you will guide them to your holy place.'*[7]

Caleb too feels on top of the world. *'We should certainly go up and take the land for ourselves,'* he adds, wrapping his arm over Joshua's shoulders. *'We can certainly do it.'*[8]

Joshua nods: soon this heaven on earth will be theirs.

Soon; not today, like he had predicted last night.

But soon.

Strategically, Moses was right to survey enemy territory before attacking. The Israelites cannot afford any mistakes.

This is a once in a lifetime opportunity.

Any offensive should not be rushed.

Paradise is worth waiting for.

In the light of Yahweh's flames, chaos abounds. Not a soul is asleep; all are engaged in a ferocious war of words as rumours spread and multiply like a disease, unleashing a cowering fear, contaminating, choking and crushing.

'We can't attack these people; they are stronger than we are.'[9]

'They are ruthless warriors.'

'Champions of combat.'

'Bloodthirsty giants.'

'With innovative weapons.'

'And monstrous city walls.'

'We wish we had died in Egypt or in this desert.'[10]

'Let's choose a leader and go back to Egypt.'[11]

Outcast from the mayhem, Joshua and Caleb sit with legs clutched tight to their chests, weighed down by great grief. Their clothes torn, the pair tremble half-naked.

'Don't turn against Yahweh!' they had begged until their throats throbbed. *'Don't be afraid of the people in that land! We will chew them up. They have no protection but* Yahweh *is with us.'*[12]

But they may as well have been shouting to an empty desert.

And now the verdict, the final judgement of Yahweh, has been delivered. For the next forty years the fire and smoke presence of Yahweh will be staying put. As requested by the masses, there will be no advance on Canaan. This entire generation of Israelites - all except young Joshua and Caleb - have squandered their chance of paradise.

Slumped beside a pile of rotting fruit, meaningless mementos from a rejected better world, Joshua picks up a pomegranate and in an eruption of fury, hurls the fruit far into the desert. The explosion, the splattered mess, the waste of such precious juice - for Joshua this sums it all up. His generation has thrown away the chance of eating such succulent fruit every day.

They have flung paradise through the air; and have themselves come crashing down in the desert. Postponed for forty years, the great homecoming has been cancelled.

The wait for heaven on earth goes on.

1. Exodus 13:21
2. Numbers 11:31
3. Genesis 9:24
4. Genesis 42:5
5. Exodus 17:13
6. Exodus 15:11

7. Exodus 15:13
8. Numbers 13:30
9. Numbers 13:31
10. Numbers 14:2
11. Numbers 14:4
12. Numbers 14:7-9

3.07 – He Meets a Man

East of the Jordan River,[1] an elderly man steps forward onto an elevated rocky plateau and an almighty army falls perfectly silent. Overwhelmed with respect, no one wants to miss a word from their one hundred and twenty year old leader.

Moses clears his throat. For forty years, he has been preparing for this: his farewell speech, the speech that will shape his legacy. If he is nervous, it doesn't show.

'Yahweh *your God has made you grow,*' the great leader begins. '*There are as many of you as there are stars in the sky.*'[2]

We immediately nod in appreciation. This is a stirring start. By referencing Yahweh's foundational promise to Abraham, Moses is bringing significance to this entirely new, young and inexperienced generation.

'*You are the children of* Yahweh,' continues Moses, his voice reverberating off the mountains and across the open expanse. '*He has chosen you from all the people on earth to be his very own.*[3] *Know in your heart that* Yahweh *corrects you as a parent corrects a child.*'[4]

Recently, we have been struck by a sickness in our stomach, shaken by the punishments that made Yahweh more akin to a tyrannous dictator than a compassionate lover.

But Moses' perspective stills our stomach.

To him, these were the actions of a parent correcting a child.

'You have had everything you needed,'[5] Moses adds. *'Neither your clothes nor sandals wore out.'*[6]

What's more, according to a note on the wall, the Israelite population only shrank slightly during four decades in barren desert. Astonishing. This is a clear testament to Yahweh's continuing care. Throughout a long and enduring punishment, God clearly did not abandon his children.

'Love Yahweh *your God with all your heart, all your soul and all your strength.*[7] He *did not care for you and choose you because there are many of you - you are the smallest nation of all. But* he *chose you because he loved you, and he kept his promise to your ancestors.'*[8]

Our stomach stills further.

Moses' words soothe us.

Alongside the text we find a map outlining the Israelites' recent travels. Instead of heading north and entering Canaan by its mountainous south, they journeyed east through Edom then north into Moab. It's not the route that we would have taken - it's longer and leaves the Israelites still needing to cross a large river - but we are not too concerned.

What is really holding our attention is a comment on the map about Edom: Moses says that God gave this land to the descendants of Esau.[9] In Phase Two, Esau sold his inheritance rights to his younger sibling Jacob, now known as Israel. In doing so, he threw away his rights to the land of Canaan.

But the nation of Esau still exists. God gave Esau's descendants the land of Edom, south east of Canaan.

Which intrigues us: God's actions seem to be stretching far beyond the text displayed in this Headquarters. Like tributaries of a mighty river, the Rescue Mission has undocumented subplots.

'Today I ask heaven and earth to be my witness. I am offering you life or death, blessings or curses. Now, choose life![10] *Pay careful attention to all the words I have said,'* concludes Moses, the volume of his voice reaching a crescendo. *'These should not be unimportant words for you, but rather they mean life to you!'*[11]

'Choose life, like Moses,' Abba pleads passionately. 'Basking in our presence, Moses has become a glorious example of humanity's great potential.'

'Even so, it wouldn't be wise - it wouldn't be fair - to ask Moses to fight in the battles awaiting across the Jordan River. Father, it is time to appoint Joshua as leader.'

Abba's eyes are ablaze. 'Joshua... Yeshua... Yesu... Jesu... Jesus... each name means "Yahweh saves."'

Father and Son look into each other's eyes; reflected back they see the love they both feel.

'Father, at Sinai our children asked not to look at *"this terrible fire anymore"... What they have said is good.*[12] Our flames may show that we are alive and animated but they are hardly relational. Who can have a relationship with flames?'

'Absolutely. Soon, Yeshua, we will have a presence on earth that our children can eat, laugh and chat with.'

Abba and Yeshua join hands and watch on utterly absorbed as Ruach and Moses climb high into Mount Nebo. Stepping onto a rocky plateau, Moses gazes out across a gloriously green fertile land, the land *promised to Abraham, Isaac and Jacob.*[13]

'*My Spirit shall not remain in human beings forever,'* Ruach whispers with gentle animation, '*they will live only one hundred and twenty years.'*[14]

Abba and Yeshua smile expansively, recognising the significance of their Lover's words; once stained in the most searing of pains, today they are painted with pride.

Helping Moses to his knees, Ruach tenderly rests the great leader's head down on the rocks; and together, the pair lay mesmerised by paradise.

Tantalisingly close to Moses' life ambition.

So close they can smell it.

Then Ruach rises like a dove.

And Moses breathes out for one final time.[15]

Fifteen hundred years later.

Dressed *in heavenly glory.*[16]

Moses finally enters the Promised Land.

And in the nation of Israel, he meets a man named Jesus.

1. Deuteronomy 1:5
2. Deuteronomy 1:10
3. Deuteronomy 14:1-2
4. Deuteronomy 8:5
5. Deuteronomy 2:7
6. Deuteronomy 29:5
7. Deuteronomy 6:5
8. Deuteronomy 7:7
9. Deuteronomy 2:4
10. Deuteronomy 30:19
11. Deuteronomy 32:46-47
12. Exodus 32:32
13. Deuteronomy 34:4
14. Genesis 6:3
15. Deuteronomy 34:5
16. Luke 9:31

3.08 – Phase Three is Complete

Swords slice limbs.

Smoke chokes lungs.

Flames char flesh.

The limbs, lungs and flesh of innocent screaming children.

Locked in intimate embrace, trembling with grief, sick to the stomach, tears stream from the eyes of Yeshua, Ruach and Abba. The sights and sounds of these sacrificed children, these so-called acts of 'worship' to please and appease Canaanite gods, rip at Elohim's heart.

To an outsider, like an Israelite, Canaan might seem civilised and advanced. The nation has prospered in the textile and timber trades, and boasts sophisticated fortified cities with water supplies and drainage. An outsider might be tempted to think that Canaan's gods deserve respect for such success. In fact, the Israelites might even wonder whether Canaan's gods aren't too dissimilar from theirs.

After all, Canaan's father of all gods is called El.

And their most active god is named Baal, meaning 'Lord.'

But scratch a bit deeper, like the Community of Elohim do, and tears begin to fall. These gods, these constructions of the human imagination, couldn't be more different from Elohim's loving embrace. Trust in these gods has led to a culture of child sacrifice, savage barbaric violence, and rampant, demeaning sex.

Even sex with relatives and animals.[1]

Growing up in the desert, Abba's children have been protected, unexposed to these practices. Yet already, whilst travelling towards Canaan, Israelites have slept with Moabites and begun to worship Baal.[2] Yahweh's covenant partner, Yahweh's shining light to the nations, has already stepped onto a slope which descends into a debilitating darkness.

Where child sacrifice is commonplace.

Normal and accepted.

'Don't learn to do the hateful things the other nations do,' Moses cried with unerring urgency during his farewell speech. *'Don't let anyone among you offer a son or daughter as a sacrifice in the fire...* Yahweh *hates anyone who does these things. Because the other nations do these things* Yahweh *will force them out of the land ahead of you.'*[3]

For centuries, Love has been holding back punishment on Canaan,[4] patiently longing and hoping for some chink of light, some glimmer of original beauty that would cause Canaan's numerous nationalities to recognise the horror of their actions.

The light never emerged.

Child sacrifices persisted.

Now all hope has faded to black.

The embracing Elohim roars out in excruciating agony as the earth shudders and shakes with ferocious rage, flinging gushing waves high into the air; and in a scene echoing their parents' momentous escape from Egypt, astonished Israelites cross the formidable Jordan River *on dry land.*[5]

Next, all who are willing and able,[6] stand ready to fight, *dressed for war.*[7] *'When you march up to attack a city, first make them an offer of peace,'* Joshua instructs. *'But if they do not make peace with you,* the city will be given to you.'*[8]

The fledgling army encircles the perimeter walls of Jericho, a monumental city on top of a hill, and for seven days they wait. When no acceptance of peace, no semblance of repentance arises, the earth begins to tremble and quake as another excruciating cry grieves the great darkness; and Jericho's walls crash to the ground.[9]

'Completely destroy these people,' Joshua roars as pandemonium ensues. *'Otherwise, they will teach you what they do for their gods.'*[10]

Swords slice limbs.

Smoke chokes lungs.

Flames char flesh.

Mourning their loss, feeling the full agony of the bloodshed, Yeshua, Ruach and Abba grip each other tight. To have to resort to such destruction hurts Love to the core. But, looking into each other's eyes, seeing the tears stream, the trio know that this pain today is necessary; eradicating the spine-chilling practice of child sacrifice, this is another step towards restoring creation to its originally intended paradise.

Elohim watches on intently as Joshua leads his army on an intelligent, sweeping offensive. Heading west then south, the Israelites discover a land in economic and political turmoil - a direct consequence of Egypt's humiliation four decades ago - and at times their conquests are straightforward.

Canaan's fortified cities, however, present a much tougher challenge. To conquer the city of Ai - near to Bethel - Joshua implements a shrewd and incisive ambush, luring the enemy out into attack, exposing their fortress to infiltration.[11]

Having previously lived in Ai and Bethel themselves, Abraham and Jacob would be particularly proud of their descendants' slick and sophisticated success. Moses, too, would be delighted to see his desert dwellers discarding their portable tents, and setting up residence in paradise: a *land with rivers and pools of water, with springs that flow in the valleys and hills, a land that has wheat and barley, vines, fig trees, pomegranates, olive oil and honey;* a land where *'you will have everything you need.'*[12]

From suffering in slavery to possessing eutopia, from submission and shame to receiving respect,[13] Phase Three is complete.

But the Rescuer's ambitions do not end there.

During the absolute anarchy of Jericho's demise, a Canaanite prostitute - a symbol of the city's promiscuous culture - was rescued.[14] Pulled out from the engulfing flames, Rahab's surprising redemption epitomises the task appointed to Israel in Phase Four.

Israel has been blessed to be a blessing; rescued to bring rescue; loved to love.

They must tell the world of Yahweh's great marriage proposal. They must share their invitation to be the Bride in God's glorious wedding.

Because when the whole earth is united in intimacy with its Lover, there will be no more pain; no more war, discrimination or destruction.

Every tear is wiped away.

1. Leviticus 18:23-24
2. Numbers 25:1-3
3. Deuteronomy 18:9-13
4. Genesis 15:16
5. Joshua 3:17
6. Deuteronomy 20:8
7. Joshua 4:12
8. Deuteronomy 20:10-13
9. Joshua 6:20
10. Deuteronomy 20:16-18
11. Joshua 8:19
12. Deuteronomy 8:7-9
13. Joshua 5:9
14. Joshua 6:2

PHASE FOUR

4.01 – Violence is Spiralling

Self-consciousness is a powerful thing.

Outwardly, we are straining to portray a smile.

Inwardly, we are riddled with doubt.

The trouble is, we have heard it all before. *'We will never stop following* Yahweh *to serve other gods!'*[1] the Phase Three wall concluded; but similar Israelite promises have been repeatedly - and rapidly - broken. Perhaps we wouldn't be so sceptical if Canaan wasn't still a cosmopolitan hotbed of competing cultures; if the Rescuer's ambition for a completely new and fresh society, free from the shackles of the old ways, had actually been realised.

But it hasn't.

A map on the wall shows us that at the time of Joshua's death, Sidonians, Mesopotamians, Amorites, Canaanites, Perizzites, Hivites, Jebusites, Ammonites, Hittites, Moabites, Edomites, Amalekites and Philistines all live interwoven among Israel's twelve tribes.

An optimist might argue that this presents an ideal opportunity to progress Yahweh's Phase Four aspirations. Surrounded by so many nationalities, here is a chance to share Yahweh's progressive desires for society.

A society with justice at its core.

A society where violence never spirals out of control.

A society where revenge is restricted by the principle of *life for life, eye for eye, tooth for tooth, hand for hand, foot for foot, burn for burn, wound for wound and bruise for bruise.*[2]

But what if Yahweh's covenant partner fails to stand out from the crowd? What if Abba's Bride becomes attracted to the contrasting and constricting ways of Baal? What if she becomes like her neighbours, lashing out spontaneously, ignoring 'eye for an eye'?

Won't they drag Yahweh down with them?

United in relationship, aren't the two inextricably linked? Don't the actions of one directly affect the reputation of the other?

By aligning himself with the Israelites, Yahweh's name could become a laughing-stock.

It could become a by-word for humiliation.

For failure.

Sweat slides from our armpits.

With the stakes so high - and when equipped with such power - it horrifies us to think that God could have taken such a risk.

But this is Love.

And Love trusts.

Love hands over its heart.

Love draws alongside.

Love sees potential.

Because Love desires, Love requires, relationship.

With the realisation refreshing us like rippling rain, we turn to our right to face the wall of Phase Four. To our surprise, apart from a few posters on the far side, the wall is mostly empty. Even a sturdy wooden desk, with chair tucked beneath, has nothing on it. All we can find is a small metallic torch in one of the desk's drawers. We swiftly pocket the torch; it could come in handy. After all, it will be getting dark soon and the limp light fitting, dangling from the ceiling, holds no bulb.

Then we see it.

Directly above our head: a hatch.

A square doorway with, 'Phase Four,' etched upon it.

Adrenaline takes hold and our tiring muscles experience resurgence. In a flash we lift the chair onto the desk, clamber up, push open the hatch and pull our re-energised frame up through the opening.

The disconcerting darkness, the puffs of rising dust, the clinging cobwebs, the clammy damp, and a reek worse than the sweat of our armpits, all stun simultaneously, causing us to cough and splutter and fall over in a heap. Slumped in the darkness, apprehensive and alone, we cannot help but wonder whether climbing inside this hatch was a terrible mistake.

Then we remember the torch. Sending forth a narrow beam, it reveals a loft filled with hanging narratives and diagrams. Not knowing where to begin, we brush away the cobwebs and flash the torch onto pages closest to us:

The *children grew up and did not know* Yahweh *or what he had done for Israel. So they did what* Yahweh *said was wrong, and they worshipped the Baal idols.*[3]

Our every muscle clenches.
We flick the torch elsewhere:

'Get that woman for me!' muscular Samson commands. *'She is the one I want!'*[4]
Within days, the privileged Israelite is marrying his Philistine bride.
But at his wedding feast, Samson is humiliated.
So he storms out and kills thirty Philistines.
So the Philistines give Samson's wife *to his best man.*[5]
So Samson ties torches to three hundred foxes and lets them loose on Philistine crops.
So the Philistines burn *Samson's wife and her father to death.*[6]
So Samson grabs a donkey's jawbone and pounds and pummels one thousand Philistines.

We shudder.
Cultures are merging.
An 'eye for an eye' is being ignored.
Violence is spiralling.
Escalating.
To barbaric proportions.
Reluctantly, we pull the torch to our right:

A Benjaminite gang rape a woman, *all night long.*[7]
Then leave her to die.
Seeking vengeance, soldiers from all over Israel converge on the rapists' home; and in a long and merciless war, ninety thousand lose their lives.
With every Benjaminite city, and every inhabitant, burnt to cinders.[8]

Gripping our scalp tight, our hands plough through our hair then fall flat over our face. Instead of looking outward and spreading peace, Israel has caved in on itself in civil war.
By partnering and aligning with this self-combusting rabble, we cannot help but wonder whether Love has in fact made a terrible mistake.

1. Joshua 24:16
2. Exodus 21:24-25
3. Judges 2:10
4. Judges 14:3
5. Judges 14:20
6. Judges 15:5-6
7. Judges 19:25
8. Judges 20:48

4.02 – It's All About Character

Stirred with compassion and overflowing with affection, a shape of majestic beauty draws close to an elderly man and, like a passionate lover, wraps over his body.

'They want a king,' the man cries until veins protrude through his skin. 'I'm so sorry. *They want a king to rule over us like all the other nations.*'[1]

'Samuel, Samuel,' Ruach whispers in pure, golden tones. Though Samuel cannot see his comforter, her presence and voice are unmistakable. *'They have not rejected you. They have rejected me from being their king. They are doing as they have always done. When I took them out of Egypt, they left me and served other gods.'*[2]

Fully present with Ruach, yet watching on from afar, Yeshua takes Abba by the hand. 'We cannot give up on our children,' he asserts. 'Look at Samuel. Look at how his heart breaks like ours.'

Deep in thought, Abba nods. 'But should we give them a king?'

Yeshua pauses.

'Remember brave Gideon. Remember how he declined his opportunity to rule, declaring instead, "Yahweh *will be your ruler*!"[3] Gideon gave us a glimpse of a glorious future where we are hailed as King.'

'But right now, anarchy reigns; *everyone* does *what seems right*.[4] How can we govern when we are so rarely invited to speak?[5] How can we rule while we are so frequently ignored? These people... they... they need a king.'

'Well, we promised Abraham that kings would come from him.[6] And other nations, like Edom, have had kings for centuries.[7] It's just that we don't want Israel to be like Edom or any other nation. We want Israel to be *a light to the nations*,[8] influencing Edom.'

'If the king *is a man after* our *own heart*,[9] if the king welcomes Ruach's inspiration, Israel can still stand out; justice and peace can still flow through our children's veins.'

'With Ruach's help, Samuel, Deborah and Gideon ushered in decades of peace for their tribes. A king could do the same for the whole nation, uniting the fragmented tribes, reminding them of our rescue, our Love.'

'But what if the king ignores Ruach and manipulates the power for his gain? A king could rob and enslave his nation... our nation.'[10]

'Character,' Abba says longingly. 'It's all about character.'

Father and Son lock eyes and exchange a proud smile.

'Son, we *do not see the same way people see.*[11] Let us choose a king from the crushed cities of Benjamin, opening the way for restoration and redemption.'

Yeshua nods.

'Let us anoint Saul: *there* is *no better Israelite than he.*'[12]

United in their choice, Ruach caresses Samuel's aching limbs, soothing and rejuvenating. '*I will send you a man from the land of Benjamin,'* she whispers in his ear. *'Appoint him to lead my people.'*

Samuel looks up, his eyes wide with surprise.

A King?

For Israel?

'Yes, precious Samuel. *I have seen the suffering of my people, and I have listened to their cry.'*[13]

Furious, bewildered, despairing, Saul's thoughts are roaming wild, rapid and free. For nearly three decades he has reigned over Israel, giving his all to the cause, winning victories *against Israel's enemies all around.*[14]

But for what?

Nothing.

Nothing except criticism.

Silence.

Abandonment.

Rejection.

From God himself.

'*What pleases* Yahweh *more,'* Samuel told Saul, *'burnt offerings and sacrifices or obedience to his voice? It is better to obey than to sacrifice… You have rejected* Yahweh's *command. Now he rejects you as king.'*[15]

The outrage, the injustice of it all, infuriates Saul to his very core. Of course, he hasn't been a perfect King. But who would have been?

Yes, it was wrong to forbid his army to eat prior to combat.[16]

Yes, it was wrong to lie about not killing all the Amalekites' cattle.[17]

Yes, it was embarrassing when his army scarpered like little children.[18]

But they were fighting Philistines! What more could they do against an army that crushed the entire Hittite Empire; against an army wielding weapons made from iron?

And now Saul's soldiers are locked in a longstanding stalemate with their fiercest foe. Positioned on opposite sides of a wide-reaching valley, neither army can attack without leaving themselves exposed. Which is why, forty days ago, the Philistines proposed a one-on-one, winner-takes-all combat.

Israel's greatest warrior shall take on Goliath.

Philistia's giant.

Philistia's three metre freak.

Saul clenches his teeth, fighting back the tears. He rolls up his fists, and stamps his feet, so as to transmit strength not weakness. For forty days, he has offered wealth, exemption from taxes, even a wife.[19]

But to no avail.

All are cowering.

Every waking hour, Saul is haunted by the knowledge that he is the obvious choice to fight Philistia's giant. Not only is he King, but Saul stands *a head taller than any other man in Israel.*[20]

Saul is Israel's giant.

The inaugural King sighs: how much longer can he delay the inevitable?

Defer the day of his final humiliation?

His crushing disfigurement.

His mangled and bloody end.

Saul rocks his head back and curses aloud. Why should he be forever remembered as the ruler responsible for plunging Israel back into slavery - a tear finally breaks through Saul's barricaded exterior - as the ruler responsible for reversing the success of Moses' Egyptian liberation?

1. 1 Samuel 8:5
2. 1 Samuel 8:7-8
3. Judges 8:23
4. Judges 21:25
5. 1 Samuel 3:1
6. Genesis 17:6
7. Genesis 36:31
8. Isaiah 51:4 (NIV)
9. 1 Samuel 13:14 (NIV)
10. 1 Samuel 8:17
11. 1 Samuel 16:7
12. 1 Samuel 9:2
13. 1 Samuel 9:16
14. 1 Samuel 14:47
15. 1 Samuel 15:22-23
16. 1 Samuel 14:24
17. 1 Samuel 15:9
18. 1 Samuel 13:7
19. 1 Samuel 17:25
20. 1 Samuel 9:2

4.03 – Decapitate His Nemesis

On the brink of Saul's battle with Goliath, the hanging text stops abruptly. The cloth is torn, either deliberately ripped, or frayed with age. Eager to learn of Saul's fate we jump forward to the next hanging cloth.

Instantly our head shakes, not quite believing what we are reading. Saul's decapitated body is nailed to the enemy's city walls. His armour is on display like a trophy in the temple of Ashtoreth,[1] a god of rising popularity throughout the nations.

'No,' we gasp almost inaudibly. 'No, no.'

It cannot be.

The Philistines have conquered Israel.

And Ashtoreth is lauding victory over Yahweh.

Feeling empty and numb, like we have reached the end of the road, we slowly fall to our knees and close our eyes.

Huddled together, united as one, Ruach, Yeshua and Abba journey down into their vast valley of pain.

'I am sorry that I made Saul king, because he has stopped following me.'[2]

'We need to find a new king. Israel needs a new king.'

'But is there anyone who still loves us? Anyone who truly - trusts us with their whole life - loves us?'

Ruach's question cracks like a thunderbolt, pinpointing the heart of the Lovers' agony.

Silence ensues as the trio bow their heads and hang in the depths of their heartbreak.

When eventually the Community of Elohim looks back, up into each other's eyes, their faces emit solidarity, determination and optimism.

'The new king,' Ruach declares, 'should be someone who has connected with our love for all nations. My Loves, listen to David on the hills of Bethlehem! Listen to the shepherd boy sing, "Yahweh, *your name is the most wonderful name in all the earth*,"[3] "*the heavens tell the glory of God, and the skies announce what his hands have made*."'[4]

'Simply stunning. This boy possesses a global perspective because his great-great-grandmother was Rahab, the Canaanite rescued from Jericho.'

'And he is also the great-grandson of Ruth, the Moabite who...'

'"*Where you go, I will go*."' Yeshua interrupts, quoting Ruth's promise to her mother-in-law Naomi. '"*Where you live, I will live. Your people will be my people, and your God will be my God*."'[5]

'Oh, Ruth, she was remarkable.' Abba's every breath ripples with affection. 'Having lost her husband, her strength in the midst of tragedy, her unswerving commitment...'

'In an increasingly violent Israel, Ruth's selfless loyalty shone out loud and clear.'

'And now her descendant David glistens with the same qualities.'

'Yes, Ruach, *go, appoint him, because he is the one*.'[6]

'Go, my Love, to Bethlehem.' Yeshua smiles profoundly. 'As foreign women in Israel, Rahab and Ruth could have been abused. But instead, in the little town of Bethlehem, each found sanctuary.'

With their immeasurable splendour satisfying an infinity of senses, Ruach kisses Yeshua and Abba, then glides gracefully into the distance. 'Oh, precious Bethlehem,' Elohim sings in unison, *'though you are too small to be among the army groups from Judah, from you will come one who will rule Israel for me.'*[7]

We open our eyes to find our torch shining down upon a fragment of narrative, protruding from a carpet of cobwebs. Perhaps this will reveal how Saul met his bloody demise?

In the depths of a considerable cave, one man squats in pitch-black darkness. The harrowed look in his eyes reveals a man whose very survival depends on keeping his wits sharp, on remaining one step ahead of his pursuer; but the net is closing in.

'Listen to my cry for help, my King and my God,'[8] the fugitive prays. *'Your love is wonderful… Protect me as you would protect your own eye. Hide me under the shadow of your wings. Keep me from the wicked who attack me, from my enemies who surround me.'*[9]

Time is running out. Indeed, what chance does he have when his hunter can summon an entire nation? When his pursuer is Saul, the King of Israel? And yet, deep down, the King's most wanted clings to one final hope.

Like Moses, waiting forty years in the desert, he too is waiting upon the fulfilment of a monumental promise from Yahweh. He is hiding in the desert, trusting that one day he will be crowned Israel's King.

Suddenly, David hears water, splashing, near the cave's entrance.

Ever so silently, David creeps forward, drawing out his infamous sword. This is the sword which shot David to prominence and ignited Saul's obsessive jealousy; the sword which once belonged to the formidable Goliath; the sword David used to decapitate Goliath, after toppling his foe with a single slingshot.[10]

David freezes, his heart pounding.

Here is Saul.

Illuminated in the cave's entrance.

Urinating against the rocks.

Alone.

Exposed.

Oblivious to David's proximity.

'God will ruin you forever,' David spits, eyeing down his pursuer. 'He will tear you away from the land of the living.[11] Today is the day Yahweh spoke of when he said, "I will give the enemy over to you."'[12]

With one swing of Goliath's sword, David can save his life.

Free Israel from Saul's abominable reign.

Claim his rightful throne.

And most significantly of all, exact revenge; dispense justice for the men, women, children, babies,[13] all slain - slaughtered at Saul's orders.

Massacred because of one priest's kindness towards David.[14]

David's sword rises over Saul's head, poised to decapitate his nemesis.

'KILL HIM,' we cry.

1. 1 Samuel 31:10
2. 1 Samuel 15:10
3. Psalm 8:1
4. Psalm 19:1
5. Ruth 1:16
6. 1 Samuel 16:12
7. Micah 5:2
8. Psalm 5:2
9. Psalm 17:7-9
10. 1 Samuel 17:49-51
11. Psalm 52:5
12. 1 Samuel 24:4
13. 1 Samuel 22:18
14. 1 Samuel 21:1-9

4.04 – Blood On His Hands

With David's sword hurtling toward Saul, the text draws to another tantalising halt, ripped at the crucial point. We instantly start rummaging in the mattress of cobwebs below us, searching for fallen fragments of text, desperate to discover Saul's fate.

Before long, we establish that Saul's pursuit of David persisted for many more years, eventually forcing the fugitive to flee to Philistia.[1]

Enemy territory.

The one place Saul wouldn't dare set foot.

Indeed, it was the Philistines who hunted Saul down in the thick of battle and critically wounded him, forcing Saul to fall on his own sword.[2] Yet, even then, David had to wait another seven years - and win a long, bloody civil war[3] - before eventually prising Israel's throne away from Saul's descendants.[4]

Exhausted and exasperated, we sigh heavily, causing a cloud of dust to puff up over our face. Brushing the filth from our eyes, we stare out at the derelict loft and notice a corner considerably cleaner and tidier than anywhere else. Clambering carefully across the creaking rafters, we reach a small bowl filled with miniscule yellow and brown seeds.

'The Kingdom of heaven is like a mustard seed,' reads a note attached to the bowl. *'That seed is the smallest of all seeds, but when it grows, it is one of the largest garden*

plants... big enough for the wild birds to come and build nests in its branches.'[5]

Behind the bowl, the text on the walls is undamaged and neatly arranged. Devouring the text, we learn of David leading his newly unified nation to victory over the Philistines. Then from almost nothing, like a mustard seed, Israel's dominion begins to expand and flourish. The acquisition of highly prized copper and iron, and the capture of key trade routes - including ports along the Mediterranean coast - quickly turns David's Kingdom into a wealthy economic force. Soon the surrounding nations are seeking sanctuary in Israel's blossoming branches and David is governor over one of the world's largest Empires.

Stunned, we lift our hands in celebration.

Out of the blue, here is the news we've been waiting for.

David has accomplished the mission of Joshua.

Completed the rescue of Moses.

And brought respect.

And influence.

To the covenant partner of Yahweh.

At long last, Israel is beginning to fulfil Yahweh's great promise to Abraham that the entire earth would be blessed through him.[6] Free from the threat of others, Israel is starting to love their neighbour.[7]

Or 'love their enemy',[8] as it says on a note beside the bowl.

Then we spot the word 'covenant'. Here on the wall is another crucial, integral, indelible promise, critical for shaping the Rescue Mission's future. We lean forward in anticipation, eager to absorb the full weight of each word.

'I will make one of your sons the next king',[9] Yahweh assures David.

'His kingdom will last before me like the sun.
It will continue forever, like the moon,
Like a dependable witness in the sky.'[10]

We stagger back in shock.

Forever!

The Kingdom of David's descendants will last forever?!

For the first time in these Headquarters, it dawns on us that these ancient narratives could actually be reaching out to us, connecting to the here and now.

To our life.

To our world.

Which leaves us wondering: three millennia after the life of David, where is David's Kingdom now? Which of his descendants is King?

Rising and falling, twisting and turning, Ruach, Abba and Yeshua dance in perfect, divine harmony.

'Gates, open wide all the way.
Open wide, aged doors
So the glorious King will come in.'

Abba's glistening melody leaves Ruach in raptures.

'Who is this glorious King?'
'Yahweh All-powerful -
He is the glorious King.'[11]

Unable to contain the revelation racing within him, Yeshua sings, '*I am the descendant from the family of David.*[12] As I ride into the City of David, with gates open wide, the euphoric crowds shall cheer, "*God bless the King of Israel!*"'[13]

The resplendent Elohim spins with infinite joy.

'Oh Abba, David deserves to receive our everlasting legacy. Like Abraham and Moses, David has never stopped trusting us.'

'Yes, *I have found in David son of Jesse the kind of man I want.*[14] Even when he was young, David roared at Goliath, "*You come to me using a sword and two spears. But I come to you in the name of* Yahweh *All-powerful.*"'[15]

Ruach twirls elegantly, pulling her partners into an intimate hold. 'Remember when David's sword was raised high over Saul, ready to kill. Remember how he felt my breath in his lungs and his arm snatched. The blade clipped Saul's robe. But no more.'

'David turned his other cheek to vengeance,'[16] beams Yeshua. 'He refused to repay evil with evil, resisting the urges inflamed within him.'

As the sun sets on a warm spring evening, Israel's King cannot resist the urges inflamed within him. Blown away by Bathsheba's breathtaking beauty, David chooses to sleep with a married woman.[17]

For several weeks, the King's scandalous secret remains safe.

Until Bathsheba reveals that she is pregnant.

Frantic.

Panicked.

Desperate to conceal his affair.

David arranges for her husband to be killed.

Israel's King becomes a murderer, with blood on his hands.

1. 1 Samuel 27:1
2. 1 Samuel 31:4
3. 2 Samuel 3:1
4. 2 Samuel 2:10
5. Matthew 13:31
6. Genesis 12:3
7. Leviticus 19:18
8. Matthew 5:44
9. 2 Samuel 7:12
10. Psalm 89:36-37
11. Psalm 24:9-10
12. Revelation 22:16
13. John 12:13
14. Acts 13:22
15. 1 Samuel 17:45
16. Matthew 5:39
17. 2 Samuel 11:4

4.05 – The Dwelling of Yahweh

Surrounded full-circle by absolute splendour, the King of Israel can hardly breathe, let alone move. The son of David and Bathsheba stands transfixed, mesmerised by the sheer extent of the beauty around him. Solomon feels like a child immersed in a story, gazing into another world. Only this world is actual, factual, real, physical, here, now, glistening in the finest gold, brimming in meticulously crafted bronze. This is a world like none ever seen before; a vista more elegant, more magnificent, more heart-stopping than even the great pyramids of Egypt; a piece of heaven on earth, a creation fit for the Creator, a house ready for the dwelling of Yahweh.

If only his father was here to see this; he would be so proud. David had worked tirelessly in preparation for this day, modelling his plans on the Tabernacle of Moses, acquiring all the stone, iron, and cedar wood required for construction.[1]

Solomon drops his head.

It just isn't fair.

His father should be here.

By the time David died, Israel was at peace with its neighbours. Free from the fear of attack, Solomon has governed over a unified society flourishing in creativity and discovery, productivity and development. By moving Israel's capital city into recently captured territory, David helped quell a sense that his own tribe Judah was superior. High on a hill and visible for miles around, Jerusalem was a city that the whole of Israel could be proud of.

And yet, despite these remarkable feats, David was forbidden from being here today.

It just isn't fair.

What more did his father have to do?

Of course David wasn't perfect. But he did face up to his faults, crying, *'Take away my sin,*[2] *save me from the guilt of murder.'*[3] And for the rest of his days he sang of the forgiveness he received,[4] claiming that he had been washed whiter than snow, proclaiming that Yahweh *'will not reject a heart that is broken and sorry for sin.'*[5] David longed for the rest of the world to know this merciful and forgiving, faithful and loving God.[6] He even believed that the Temple would advance one of Yahweh's deepest desires: dwelling on Earth.

And yet, despite all this, David was forbidden from building Jerusalem's Temple in his lifetime.

And why? Because David had *fought many wars* and *killed many people.*[7] And Yahweh wanted the foundations of his residence on Earth to be peace and unity, not bloodshed and war.

Solomon grinds his teeth, infuriated by the insanity, the indignity, the injustice of it all. What more did his father have to do?

Oh, how David would have loved to have seen today's grand opening. Jerusalem's Temple will further unite his nation around their shared history and common purpose. It shall stand as a permanent, inescapable

reminder of Yahweh's desired intimacy with Israel.
'I will live among the Israelites in this Temple, and I will never leave my people,' Yahweh promised Solomon.
If...
If...
'If you obey all my laws and commands.'[8]
The condition has vibrated through Solomon like a clanging cymbal, reminding him of Israel's repeated neglect of Yahweh's commands. Taking their prosperity for granted, they even lost the wooden box that the laws were kept in.[9] Which is why Solomon's heart is pounding as the rescued Ark of the Covenant is carried into the heart of the Temple, restoring it to its rightful place in the Holy of Holies.[10]

All of a sudden the entire Temple is encompassed within a mighty swirling cloud as Ruach dances and sprints and soars, enveloping all within the Shekinah, the visible presence of Yahweh. Solomon is no longer frozen to the spot. He is spinning around with arms raised high, feeling as if he is flying; as if he has taken hold of Ruach's hand and is soaring around the Temple with her. This love he feels is like none he has ever experienced before. This love is uncomplicated, uncluttered, a love with no ulterior motive.

And for the first time in his life Solomon truly appreciates the desire for exclusivity in relationship. At last he grasps why Yahweh's first command was, *'You must not have any other gods except me.'*[11] And why, why, why would anyone choose any other god - a god chiselled from wood - when Yahweh is like this?

Alive.

Near.

Tangible.

Visible.

Soothing.

Exhilarating.

'Yahweh', Solomon announces, *'I have truly built a wonderful Temple for you - a place for you to live forever.'*[12]

Ruach stops in her tracks. The Shekinah hovers over Solomon, utterly captivated by his words - words spoken as if Solomon is conversing with a lifelong friend. *God's people are in his presence,*[13] and the Community of Elohim spins head over heels, dizzy with exhilaration.

'Solomon's name means peace,' explains Yeshua, speaking as a Groom caressing his Bride. 'Jerusalem, you are the foundations of peace. You are the light of the world, a city *on a hill* that *cannot be hidden.'*[14]

'Foreigners from other lands will hear about your greatness', Solomon responds. *'They will come from far away to pray at this Temple.'*[15] And sure enough, when the Queen of Sheba travels for many months to see Jerusalem's Temple - when she concludes, *'Praise* Yahweh, he *has constant love for Israel'*[16] - the embracing Elohim beams in sheer euphoria.

Until... until jaws drop in shock.

And horror.

And devastated sorrow.

When *on a hill east of Jerusalem, Solomon* builds *two places for worship.*

One for *Chemosh, the hated god of the Moabites.*
The other for *Molech, the hated god of the Ammonites.*[17]

1. 1 Chronicles 22:2–4
2. Psalm 51:7
3. Psalm 51:14
4. Psalm 32:5
5. Psalm 51:17
6. Psalm 86:9–15
7. 1 Chronicles 22:8
8. 1 Kings 6:12–13
9. 1 Samuel 4:11
10. 1 Kings 8:6
11. Exodus 20:3
12. 1 Kings 8:13
13. 1 Kings 7:48
14. Matthew 5:14
15. 1 Kings 8:41–42
16. 1 Kings 10:9
17. 1 Kings 11:7

4.06 – After the Affair

'Arghhh, Solomon,' we scream at the top of our voice. 'Solomon, Solomon, what are you doing? If the Shekinah of Yahweh was indeed so real, so alive, so near, tangible and visible, soothing and exhilarating, why, why, why would you build shrines to other gods? Ohhh, Solomon, what are you doing?!'

The next narrative on the wall is covered by an additional extract, presumably torn from elsewhere.

'Go and marry an unfaithful woman and have unfaithful children,' the extra text reads, *'because the people in this country have been completely unfaithful to* me.'[1]

This is chilling.

Unnerving.

Heart-wrenching.

God is asking a man named Hosea to wholeheartedly and exclusively commit himself to a prostitute, a woman who is highly unlikely to return his affection, a woman who will carry on sleeping around with other men. And why? Because this woman's betrayal of Hosea will illustrate Israel's unfaithfulness to Yahweh.

'My people ask wooden idols for advice,' says Yahweh.
'Like prostitutes, they have chased after other gods.
And have left their own God.'[2]

Israel has been like a married prostitute. And whenever Hosea returns home to find his wife in bed with another man, he will be sharing in the heartbreak that Yahweh feels.

Oh, Solomon, Solomon, what are you doing?

Solomon, you are being unfaithful to Yahweh.

Solomon, you are sleeping around with other gods.

Solomon, you are acting like your father when he met your mother.

Solomon, you are having an affair.

Perhaps the anger that we feel - perhaps that's something of God's anger? After all, it's not like Yahweh hasn't been betrayed before. When the golden calf was built at the foot of Mount Sinai, when the liberated Israelites announced, *'These are your gods who brought you out of Egypt,'*[3] God's heartbroken fury killed three thousand people.

What will the consequences be this time?

We tear off the Hosea narrative and tentatively peer beneath.

Returning home from a life on the run, feeling like Moses about to confront Pharaoh, Jeroboam strides towards Israel's King, on a mission to liberate.

To put an end to widespread suffering.

Oppression.

Persecution.

Slavery.

All within Israel itself.

All consequences - terrifying legacies - of Solomon's devastating reign.[4]

'Remember you were slaves in Egypt,'[5] Moses used to implore his liberated Israelites.

But Solomon forgot Moses' plea.

Solomon sentenced vast numbers to decades of back-breaking labour.[6]

'The king must not have too many horses for himself,' Moses cried, *'he must not send people to Egypt to get more horses, because the Lord has told you, "Don't return that way again"'.*[7]

But Solomon had *twelve thousand horses*.[8]

He *even imported horses from Egypt*.[9]

God's rescued ones were returning to the home of their enslavement. They were furthering their military might; adding to their arsenal.

Extending their ability to intimidate.

To impose.

Enforce.

Enslave.

When Jeroboam first confronted Solomon all those years ago, he was hounded into exile. Fleeing for his life, he found refuge in Egypt.[10] Now, with Solomon dead, Jeroboam has returned to challenge Israel's King once again.

King Rehoboam locks eyes with his father's nemesis.

'My father beat you with whips,' Rehoboam sneers, 'but my whips shall be tipped with metal.'[11]

Jeroboam's heart drops. Aghast, he turns away in anguish as he senses shards of metal shredding Israelite flesh.

Abhorrent.

Repulsive.

Revolting.

Jeroboam must revolt.

Because after the affair, comes the break up.[12]

The nation of Israel splits into two.

In all regions except David's home of Judah, the people cry, *'We have no share in David!'*[13] and Jeroboam is hailed as King.

In terms of size, economic prowess and military potential, Jeroboam's dominion is the only Israel worthy of note. Jeroboam's only shortcoming is the loss of Jerusalem's Temple. After all, where will his new Israel worship? Or more to the point, who will they worship? Jeroboam can hardly endorse a deity with an everlasting commitment to David's family.

Jeroboam needs a new god for Israel.

So he builds a golden calf.

And announces: *'Israel, here are your gods who brought you out of Egypt.'*[14]

Ruach, Yeshua and Abba bury their heads into each other's chests. Pain shooting through hearts, they find solace within their perfect community of unfaltering Love.

'My people have made up their minds to turn away from me,' says Yeshua, choking through his tears. *'Oh, Israel, how can I give you up? How can I give you away, Israel? My heart beats for you.'*[15] Israel *put on her rings and jewellery, and went chasing after her lovers, but she forgot me!'*[16]

'Oh Beautiful Yeshua, my Love, soon the prostitute will be drawn to you and her love will overflow. She will kiss your feet and wash them with her tears. She shall douse them with perfume and dry them with her hair.'[17]

Abba nods. 'Hosea's name means "rescue"; we will ask Hosea to pay the price to buy back his wife, the prostitute, from her other lovers. *In the same way I love the people of Israel*.[18] I will pay the price to restore her purity, and buy back her beauty. *I will forgive them for leaving me and will love them freely*.'[19]

Yeshua looks up, his eyes shining romantically.

'*I will make* Israel *my promised bride forever*.[20] And *in the future she will call me "my husband"*.'[21]

1. Hosea 1:2
2. Hosea 4:12
3. Exodus 32:4
4. 1 Kings 12:4
5. Deuteronomy 24:18
6. 1 Kings 9:15
7. Deuteronomy 17:16
8. 2 Chronicles 1:14
9. 2 Chronicles 1:16
10. 1 Kings 11:40
11. 1 Kings 12:14
12. 1 Kings 11:33
13. 1 Kings 12:16
14. 1 Kings 12:28
15. Hosea 11:7–8
16. Hosea 2:13
17. Luke 7:36
18. Hosea 3:1
19. Hosea 14:4
20. Hosea 2:19
21. Hosea 2:16

4.07 – Like Wild Animals

Naked and skinny and covered in flies, a group of young children clamber on top of a rubbish dump, scavenging through the filth, desperate to discover discarded scraps of meat and feed off their findings.

From the other side of the road, Amos watches the scene stunned to his core.

Heartbroken that humans could live like this.

Dumbfounded that nobody seems to care.

In the distance, Amos can see Jeroboam's golden calf - now a century and a half old - still as popular as ever. Every day, thousands of worshippers bow down before the calf, giving thanks for their ivory palaces, for their abundance of meat and wine, for security and safety, for being untouchable, for the luxury of lounging around not needing to work.[1]

The gods of Baal have been kind and generous.

They are worthy of praise.

Yet here, before Amos' eyes, are children covered in dirt, scavenging like wild animals.

How is this possible?

Poverty.

Extreme poverty.

Next to extreme luxury: decadence, breathtaking in its extravagance.

How?

Only now can Amos comprehend the devastated fury in Yahweh's voice.

God was disgusted.

Sickened.

Repulsed.

Amos shudders, whimpering nervously. Once an innocuous shepherd from the gentle countryside of Judah, now he stands as a foreigner, a tourist, in Israel's southernmost town, tasked with proclaiming Yahweh's anger. And his hosts are not going to like it. They will condemn him as a madman and arrest him as a criminal. Why, oh why, Amos wonders, should a quiet, peaceful shepherd deserve a fate like that?

Catching the eye of an abandoned child - scratched and bruised - heat stirs in Amos' heart. It swells and swells until the child holds out a begging hand, and Amos screams out in agony.

Stunned passers-by turn their heads.

Then Amos lets fly.

'This is what Yahweh *says: "For the many crimes of Israel, I will punish them. For silver, they sell people that have done nothing wrong; they sell the poor as if they were nothing, and they refuse to be fair to those that are suffering."'*

Already Bethel's streets are in uproar.

'"Listen to this funeral song that I sing about you, people of Israel.[2] You turn justice upside down, and you throw on the ground what is right.[3] You walk on poor people, forcing them to give you grain."'[4]

From an onslaught of abuse fired at Amos, one single shout stands out.

'You hypocrite! You Judean hypocrite!'

The cry stings because Amos knows it is true.

Judah is just as guilty of abusing the poor as Israel. Indeed, the very origins of Israel's breakaway from Judah are rooted in King Solomon's tyranny and point-blank hypocrisy. With his mouth Solomon would say, *'The rich and poor are alike* - Yahweh *made them all'*;[5] *'whoever mistreats the poor insults their Maker'*;[6] *'being kind to the poor is like lending to* Yahweh.'[7] But in practice, Solomon spent his days acquiring ever increasing riches, adorning his Palace with the finest golden carvings. His greed made him the wealthiest king on earth.[8]

'Listen to me,' Amos continues. *'Listen, you who walk on helpless people,* saying, *"we can charge them more and give them less, and we can change the scales to cheat the people. We will buy poor people for silver and needy people for the price of a pair of sandals."*[9] Listen! Come to Yahweh *and live, or he will move like fire against the descendants of Joseph. The fire will burn Bethel, and there will be no one to put it out.*[10] Israel will be wiped from the earth.'

As the authorities lead Amos away, he tilts his head back and screams to the skies, *'"I am giving the command to scatter the nation of Israel among all the nations."'*[11]

The raucous crowds roar with laughter.

But little does anyone realise.

Out in the east.

An Empire is on the rise.

An Empire with eyes set on world domination.

An Empire rampaging ravenously, spraying blood at will.

The Assyrian Empire stretches as far east as Babylonia, takes in the mighty Tigris and Euphrates Rivers, and now has its sights set on conquering Egypt in the west. But to reach Egypt, they must first infiltrate Israel - a nation in turmoil, a nation devoid of leadership, a nation which has had five kings in ten years after successive assassinations.

The Assyrians slay their prey with consummate ease.

Like a lion devouring a lamb, Israel is ripped to shreds. In the Law of Moses, the ultimate punishment for repeated unrepentant disobedience was to *rot away* in enemy territory.[12]

And that is what happens.

Survivors of the annihilation are enslaved and deported, scattered far and wide throughout the Empire. With their collective identity torn apart, the exiles quickly fade into obscurity.

Meaning Israel is no more.

Leaving the Rescue Mission hanging by a thread.

Judah - tiny Judah - is all that remains of the nation fathered and established by Abraham, Jacob, Moses and David.

And the bloodthirsty Assyrians are licking their lips.

Judah shall be their easiest conquest yet.

1. Amos 6:4-6
2. Amos 5:1
3. Amos 5:7
4. Amos 5:11
5. Proverbs 22:2
6. Proverbs 17:5
7. Proverbs 19:17
8. 1 Kings 10:23
9. Amos 8:2-6
10. Amos 5:6
11. Amos 9:8
12. Leviticus 26:39

4.08 – Dead

The sky hangs heavy and grey over Jerusalem, the rain powers down. And in the courtyard of Solomon's Temple, one solitary prisoner suspends shackled and shamed, head and hands locked in the stocks, blood seeping from his searing wounds.

'"*Perhaps they will listen,*"'[1] the prisoner screeches, bitterness and sarcasm scratching his throat. '"Perhaps you can save them," you told me. But I never stood a chance, did I? *Can a leopard change its spots?* They're addicted *to doing evil.*[2] *You tricked me… I have become a joke.*[3] *Why did I ever come out of the womb to see trouble and sorrow and to end my days in shame?*[4] *I don't understand why my pain has no end.*'[5]

Propelled by the relentless rain, blood skims down his cold naked body.

Jeremiah has given up living.

Jeremiah would rather be dead.

'When Judah was surrounded and they were running out of food, when destruction was imminent, oh, of course they cared about you then, Yahweh. Of course, they were grateful when you decimated the Assyrian camp, killing hundreds of thousands overnight. '"*For the sake of David,*"'[6] you rescued them. Yet in a flash they forget you. They only remember your unconditional covenant with David. They think it promises that their kingdom will go on forever. They think it guarantees them rescue from every enemy.'

Rain splashes and spits from Jeremiah's mouth.

'But they forget your conditional covenant. The one you made with Moses, where you gave us a task, a responsibility, appointing us to usher in your kingdom of peace over all the earth. Obedience promised prosperity. Disobedience: destruction.'

Thunder cracks across the skies.

'Oh, if only I could have stopped Josiah from fighting the Egyptians... He had found the lost book of Moses' laws. He had recommitted to your ways,[7] smashing the statues of the Assyrian gods. He even tore down Jeroboam's golden calf in Bethel.[8] The Assyrian stranglehold was weakening. But then...'

Squirming and shuddering, his skin scrapes across the stocks.

'...Then Josiah was killed by the Egyptians. And now our King is in an alliance with the Pharaoh. We are slaves of Egypt once again.'

Jeremiah raises his eyes to the Temple, Solomon's famous triumphant masterpiece.

'I'm sorry, Yahweh... *this place where* you *have chosen to be worshipped is nothing more than a hideout for robbers.*[9] It is filled with altars to Egyptian gods. It must break your heart. *Judah saw that* you *divorced unfaithful Israel because of her adultery,*[10] yet still we sleep around. Soon we will be offering...'

Jeremiah gasps and chokes, overwhelmed by inconsolable grief.

'...offering their gods our own children; the limbs,

lungs and flesh of innocent, screaming children. Soon our King will tie up his own son, pull down his knife and watch his own flesh and blood go up in flames. Just like King Manasseh did.[11] Just like King Ahaz.'[12]

Child sacrifice! As the horror sinks in, we kick out in rage, slamming our foot into a rafter. The whole loft shudders and a foul, dank cloud of dust showers down on our head.

Child sacrifice was supposed to have been eradicated from the earth centuries ago! That's why God allowed the Israelites to massacre the Canaanites. Yet still the ghastly slaughters go on. Even the King of Jerusalem, God's city of peace, God's light to the world, ties up his own son... a tear drips from our chin. How could humans have got it so wrong?

When God stopped Abraham from sacrificing Isaac, when God told Moses that only animals should be offered, was his message not clear enough?

Love hates the burning of children.

The Canaanites were destroyed for these crimes.

And Judah deserves to die too.

But Judah won't be destroyed; God saved them from the Assyrians and he will do it again. No matter how fierce the enemy surrounding it, no matter how much Jerusalem deserves destruction, Love - long suffering, enduring Love - will protect his city on a hill.

David's kingdom will last forever.

It's covenanted.

It's contracted.[13]

'For the sake of David': that's what's keeping the Rescue Mission alive.

To shut up Jeremiah's incessant chattering, a Temple guard steps out into the rain, strides over to his prisoner and strikes him hard across the face. Jeremiah riles and spits then slowly lifts his head and glares into his torturer's unrepentant eyes. *'Run for your lives!'* he snaps, menacingly. *'Disaster is coming.'*[14]

Elohim has been left with no other option.[15] Love's covenant partner, Love's representative on earth, has committed *more evil than the nations* God *destroyed ahead of the Israelites.*[16]

The Babylonians surround Jerusalem.

The embracing Elohim roars out in excruciating agony.

And the enemy breaks through Jerusalem's barricades.[17]

Swords slice limbs.

Smoke chokes lungs.

Flames char flesh.

Man, woman or child, the Babylonians kill at will.

First the words blur, then the wall sways.

The Rescue Mission: it's all over.

It's finished.

Dead.

All that work, all that blood, sweat and tears - Noah, Abraham, Moses, David - it's all come to nothing. Our eyes glaze over and we stumble back, arms swinging chaotically. Seeing nothing, feeling nothing but pain, we trip and, as if unconscious and fainting, crash to the dusty loft floor.

Yet still we fall.

Flying, flailing, falling through the air.

Flying.

Flailing.

Falling.

Until slam; flat solid concrete knocks us cold.

1. Jeremiah 26:2
2. Jeremiah 13:23
3. Jeremiah 20:7
4. Jeremiah 20:18 (NIV)
5. Jeremiah 15:18
6. 2 Kings 19:34–35
7. 2 Kings 23:3
8. 2 Kings 23:15
9. Jeremiah 7:11
10. Jeremiah 3:8
11. 2 Kings 21:6
12. 2 Kings 16:3
13. 1 Kings 11:36
14. Jeremiah 6:1
15. Jeremiah 9:7
16. 2 Kings 21:9
17. 2 Kings 25:10

4.09 – The Rejected Romantic

We can hear the screams.

We can see the devastation.

Tripping between blackouts and flashes of white, we see the smoke and ash swirling in the massacre's aftermath, the shrapnel and debris flying in the wind, holding no regard for the mutilated bodies in the rubble below.

'My eyes have no more tears and I am sick to the stomach. I feel empty inside because my people have been destroyed.[1] Jerusalem was once a great city among the nations, but now she is like a widow.'[2]

Our vision is blurring, fading to black, but the voice is crystal clear.

A second voice interjects, broken and choking: *'The babies are so thirsty their tongues stick to the roofs of their mouths. Children beg for bread, but no one gives them any. Those who once ate fine foods are now starving in the streets.[3] With their own hands kind women cook their own children.'[4]*

We are devoid of our senses, conscious of nothing but the voices.

'I could no longer share David's Temple with all their other lovers. I had to leave our home,[5] leave her unprotected, exposed, vulnerable. Now *the stones of the Temple are scattered at every street corner.*[6] Passers-by laugh, *"Is this the city the people called the most beautiful city, the happiest place on earth?"'*[7]

The sound of a third voice awakens our senses. It is gorgeous and diverse, shimmering like a rainbow.

'Jerusalem was our heaven on earth, the start of Eden's restoration, paradise's rescue. Now Jerusalem is a hell; a hell like Gehenna, the Valley of Hennom, the graveyard of children slaughtered *as sacrifices for Molech.*'[8]

We cannot move a muscle. We imagine the three mourners in floods of tears, locked in embrace.

'*"What can I bring before* Yahweh?"' our Bride asks. *"Should I give my first child for the evil I have done? Should I give my very own child for my sin?"*[9] No, no, no, my love, why, why, why would we seek death and bloodshed? We are not like the gods of the human imagination. We desire life. We want humans to *do what is right to other people, love being kind to others, and live humbly, obeying your God.*'[10]

'Abba, there needs to be an ultimate sacrifice to convince humans that they do not need to offer their own children as sacrifices; a definitive death to defeat *the power of sin just once - enough for all time.*'[11]

A quivering silence ensues in which we finally manage to open our eyes and establish that we are lying stretched out on a cold, concrete floor.

'*On the day you were born…*'

The floor is littered with debris, the aftermath of a considerable crash: our crash.

'*…you were thrown out into the open field, because you were hated. When I passed by and saw you kicking about in* *your blood, I said to you, "Live!" You grew up… and became like a beautiful jewel.'*

Each word feels like it is being forced out under tremendous strain.

'Later when I passed by you and looked at you, I saw that you were old enough for love. So I spread my robe over you and covered your nakedness. I also made a promise to you and entered into an agreement with you so that you became mine.'[12]

The words are flowing more easily now. And we lie mesmerised.

'I wrapped you in fine linen and covered you with silk. I put jewellery on you: bracelets on your arms, a necklace around your neck, a ring in your nose, earrings in your ears and a beautiful crown on your head. You became a queen… famous among the nations.'[13]

The intimacy.

The romance.

It only adds to the tragedy.

The tragedy of the Rescue Mission's failure.

'You took your beautiful jewellery… and you made for yourselves male idols so you could be a prostitute with them… You gave my oil and incense as an offering to them.'[14]

The beautiful Bride, crowned as a queen, chose instead to be a prostitute.

Tears dripping to the floor, we can do nothing but simply lie in the agony. We surrender to the poetry of Love, the emotion of the rejected romantic.

'You also took your sons and daughters… and you sacrificed

them to the idols as food. You killed my children and offered them up in fire.[15] *I never commanded you to do such a hateful thing. It never entered my mind that you would.'*[16]

The pain is just too much. We long to be numb again. We screw our eyes shut and our mind trips back to Gehenna, the Valley of Hennom, the graveyard of bones left drying and decaying in the midday sun.

'Valley of dry bones,' says the rainbow voice, '*I will put muscles on you and flesh on you and cover you with skin. Then I will put breath in you so you will come to life.*[17] *You will live in the land I gave to your ancestors, and you will be my people, and I will be your God.*[18] *You will say, "This land was ruined, but now it has become like the Garden of Eden."'*[19]

'From the graveyard of Gehenna to the Garden of Eden, yes Ruach my love, creation can still be restored. Soon we will live with our Bride forever in marital bliss.'

'But love remains a choice.'

'Who will want this paradise?'

'Who will choose our embrace?'

1. Lamentations 2:10–12
2. Lamentations 1:1
3. Lamentations 4:4–5
4. Lamentations 4:10
5. Ezekiel 10:18
6. Lamentations 4:1
7. Lamentations 2:15
8. Jeremiah 32:35
9. Micah 6:6–7
10. Micah 6:8
11. Romans 6:10
12. Ezekiel 16:6–8
13. Ezekiel 16:9–14
14. Ezekiel 16:17–18
15. Ezekiel 16:20–21
16. Jeremiah 32:35
17. Ezekiel 37:5
18. Ezekiel 36:28
19. Ezekiel 36:35

4.10 – The Roaring Lion

Under the full force of the lion's roar, Daniel's elderly bones feel as if they will shatter. Pinned against the wall, he fights to stay hidden in the dark, to slow the beat of his heart and quiet the fear in his breath.

The roar is still ricocheting through Daniel's body when he hears the sound that he fears the most.

The sound of a lion rising.

Prowling.

Approaching.

Daniel cannot push himself back any further into the wall. First he feels the breath, then the whiskers and mane brushing across his face. Bracing himself for the moment the lion's jaws rip apart his sagging flesh, Daniel dispenses one final frantic prayer.

'Yahweh *is my shepherd*.'[1] His *love never ends*.'[2]

A wet slobbery tongue slides across Daniel's face.

'He *will not reject his people forever*.'[3]

Another giant lick.

'*He does not like to punish people*.'[4]

Daniel dares to open up his senses: he has not been torn into a hundred mutilated pieces, he can feel no excruciating pain - and his predator is retreating.

'*I will be like a lion to Israel*,' Yahweh warned Hosea, '*I will attack them and tear them to pieces*.'[5]

Daniel slowly lowers himself to the ground, his heart pounding in the presence of Yahweh the roaring lion, destroyer of Jerusalem, the one who ripped meat from his lambs. Clutching his knees close to his chest, Daniel clings desperately to a promise embedded in the heart of every Judean exile: *'Babylon will be powerful for seventy years,'* Yahweh told Jeremiah, 'then *I will come to you* and *bring you back to Jerusalem.'*[6]

Seventy years ago, the Babylonian captors pointed at Jerusalem's decimated Temple and laughed, *'Where is your God?'*[7] It seemed as if Yahweh had left his people forever. But this was not divorce, only separation.

Already the Babylonian Empire is crumbling.

Already the Empire's king is Median, not Babylonian.

Already the heir to Judah's throne has been released from captivity.[8]

Surely it won't be long now until Jerusalem's exiles are returning home.

Even during Jerusalem's most devastating massacre, the stripped naked Bride was given an opportunity to choose life: those who surrendered without fighting would *'escape with their lives and live.'*[9]

And live they have.

Working as bankers and merchants within a thriving metropolis of trade, the Judeans have prospered to such an extent that some even began to wonder whether Yahweh was actually still with the exiles, helping them.

But that wasn't possible - was it?

The gods are fixed to certain locations - aren't they?

One god rules here.

Another god rules there.

Marduk has Babylon.

Yahweh has - had - Jerusalem.

That's just how it is.

But when Daniel and some other Judeans began to hear Yahweh speak to them in Babylon, entire worldviews began to crumble. One exile even heard, *'When you walk through fires, you will not be burnt;'*[10] and sure enough, when Hananiah, Mishael and Azariah were thrown into an enormous blazing furnace, *their hair was not burned, their robes were not burned and they did not even smell of smoke.*[11] What's more, a mysterious fourth figure was seen standing with them in the flames.

Leaving Daniel in no doubt: Yahweh was with them.

In Babylon.

In Marduk's Babylon.

'I am the true God,' proclaimed Yahweh. *'There was no God before me, and there will be no God after me.'*[12]

The thought was mind-blowing; it was the greatest ground-breaking revelation of all. But, bit by bit by bit, it began to make sense. Yahweh is not limited to one location, because Yahweh is not limited at all. Yahweh can be both the shepherd and the lion, or both the father and the husband, or the mother unable to *forget the baby she nurses.*[13]

Because Yahweh is the first God and the last God.

The one and only God, who *rules over every kingdom on earth.*[14]

Daniel stretches out his legs and marvels once more at the thought of one giant God who created the entire world peacefully, who simply spoke and there was.

If only the Babylonians knew this, perhaps they wouldn't be so violent. They think that Marduk created the world by ripping apart his rival Tiamat. Then Marduk added humans to be his slaves, to do the work that the gods did not want to do. By contrast, Yahweh invites humans to work in relationship with their Creator, sharing responsibility for the cultivation of creation.

Resting his head on the ground, Daniel makes no effort to still his racing mind. He will not sleep tonight; not while he remains a terrified lamb lying beside lions.

Nursing the restless babe in her arms, Ruach whispers, 'Thank you, my love. Thank you for not fighting back. Thank you for surrendering without violence. The path you have chosen is the only way - the only way to bring peace to earth. Beautiful Daniel, *I will not forget you. I have written your name on my hand.*[15] *Forget what happened before... look at the new thing I am going to do.*[16] *For a long time I have kept silent, I have been quiet and held myself back. But now, like a woman in childbirth, I cry out, I gasp, I pant.*[17] Like a shepherd, I will round up our scattered lambs and lead our flock home. Then the roaring lion will become a lamb.'

1. Psalm 23:1
2. Lamentations 3:22
3. Lamentations 3:31
4. Lamentations 3:33
5. Hosea 5:14
6. Jeremiah 29:10
7. Psalm 42:3
8. 2 Kings 25:27
9. Jeremiah 38:2
10. Isaiah 43:2
11. Daniel 3:26
12. Isaiah 43:10
13. Isaiah 49:15
14. Daniel 5:21
15. Isaiah 49:15-16
16. Isaiah 43:18-19
17. Isaiah 42:14 (NIV)

4.11 – Heart's Desire

Taking another sip from his wine, the King of Persia sits gazing in admiration at the most incredible woman he has ever known. Esther's breathtaking beauty is why he chose her;[1] but it is her destabilising mix of intellect, composure and kindness that keeps Xerxes' infatuation growing.

On the other side of their banquet table, the most powerful woman in the world feels powerless. Her husband's Empire may stretch from India to Egypt, dwarfing all Empires before it, but Queen Esther can feel her insides trembling.

What she is about to say could cost Esther her life.

Yet she has to try something.

She just cannot watch idly on.

While the Persians massacre all Judeans.

Annihilating *young and old.*

Women and little children too.[2]

Queen Esther takes a deep breath - before revealing her most closely guarded secret: she is herself Judean.

Xerxes is silenced.

'*My king,*' continues Esther, authoritative yet flirtatious, '*if you are pleased with me, and if it pleases you, let me live. This is what I ask. And let my people live too.*'[3]

For many minutes the King simply stares into his wife's sensational eyes. This astonishing woman never fails to slip behind his kingly exterior; Esther reminds

Xerxes that he is human. How can he possibly say no to her?

From the brink of extermination, Esther's courage transforms the Judeans' fate, ushering in *a time of happiness, joy, gladness and honour for the Jewish people.*[4] Her bravery paves the way for Mordecai - Esther's cousin and adopted father - to be crowned Persia's second most powerful man.[5] When Esther's stepson becomes Persia's next King, he permits several Judeans to return home to Jerusalem,[6] even providing funds to restore the city's former glory.[7] Indeed, Esther's heroism convinces *many people through all the empire* to become *Jews*.[8]

Relief and elation bubble within us.
This is remarkable.
Since entering the Promised Land, the Israelites have continually rejected their commission to spread Yahweh's love to all nations. Which is why, in the end, Yahweh forced them out, scattering them across the nations. So in some strange, shocking and curiously beautiful way, the Israelites' punishment for disobedience - a punishment of last resort[9] - has led to many foreign hearts ditching their idols and falling in love with Yahweh.
Destruction and exile have actually advanced the ambitions of Phase Four.
From death has come life.

Is Yahweh smiling?

Singing?

Even dancing?!

Nehemiah's imagination is running wild.

To his left is Jerusalem's rebuilt Temple; to his right, the renovated city walls. And straight ahead, every resident of Jerusalem stands in mesmeric hush, listening to Ezra recite Yahweh's laws. Everyone in the courtyard has their own personal tale of liberation and restoration, but one particular family catches Nehemiah's eye. Until recently, this family was so crippled by poverty, they had been forced to sell their children as slaves,[10] just to make ends meet.

Now, the family stands reunited.

This is what happens, Nehemiah beams, when Moses' laws are actually followed. Yahweh's instructions may be one thousand years old but they still have the potential to literally, physically, set people free.[11]

To bring equality.

To end poverty.

And offer a fresh start for all.

By cutting extortionate taxes.

By slashing the interest charged on debts.[12]

By announcing a day of Jubilee where all slaves are declared free.[13]

Nehemiah and Ezra have brought a piece of heaven back to earth.

At long last, Amos' cry for justice is being heard.

'Thank you, Yahweh,' Nehemiah whispers. 'Thank you for your *good plans for* us; plans to give us *hope and a good future.'*[14] Nehemiah pauses. He gulps. 'But you had good plans for us before, and look what happened. Jeremiah said that we were like clay in your hands. You were shaping us, moulding us, *but something went wrong.*[15] We did not want to be moulded. We rejected your plans and spun away, ending up in a horrible mess.'

Silence is stolen as an almighty celebration begins to spiral around the Temple courtyard.

'Oh Yahweh,' Nehemiah roars through the cacophony. 'This time, we choose to stay in your hands. This time craft us into a stunning masterpiece, the way you originally intended us to be.'[16]

The sound of happiness in Jerusalem is *heard far away*[17] as the whole city sings:

'*Praise God in his Temple;*
   Praise him in his mighty heaven.
Praise him for his strength;
   Praise him for his greatness...
Praise him with tambourines and dancing...
   Let everything that breathes praise Yahweh.'[18]

'*When* Yahweh *brought* us *back to Jerusalem,*
   It seemed as if we were dreaming.
Then we were filled with laughter,
   And we sang happy songs.
Then the nations said,
   "Yahweh *has done great things for them.*"'[19]

'Yahweh *has comforted his people.*
  He has saved Jerusalem.
Yahweh *will show his holy power*
  To all the nations.
Then everyone on earth
  Will see the salvation of our God.'[20]

Swept up by the swinging dance, Nehemiah can sense Yahweh's joy overflowing all around. Indeed, Ruach, Abba and Yeshua are grinning and singing, twirling in the midst of the celebrations, dancing with their heart's desire.

1.   Esther 2:17
2.   Esther 3:13
3.   Esther 7:3
4.   Esther 8:15
5.   Esther 10:3
6.   Ezra 7:13
7.   Ezra 7:20-21
8.   Esther 8:17
9.   Leviticus 26:27-35
10. Nehemiah 5:5
11. Leviticus 25:41
12. Nehemiah 5:7
13. Leviticus 25:40
14. Jeremiah 29:11
15. Jeremiah 18:4
16. Jeremiah 18:4
17. Nehemiah 12:43
18. Psalm 150:2-6
19. Psalm 126:1-2
20. Isaiah 52:9-10

PHASE FIVE

5.01 – Blasphemy

Tears tumble from Abba's distressed and torn, passionate and longing eyes. Wracked with grief, Abba's mournful gaze is fixed upon the excruciating plight of one man clothed only in blood, clinging helplessly to his final moments of life. This precious child of Abba, this masterpiece of Elohim, hangs humiliated from two rugged wooden beams, arms swept out across the horizontal, legs draped down the vertical. Drained of all energy, for one final time the man screams out. Then he is gone, breathing no more.

At the moment of loss, Abba too cries out, audibly letting loose his distress. This man now hanging limp, absent of life, was loved beyond measure. And the greatest tragedy of all is that the man never even knew it. This dearly desired, delicately crafted life fell so short of his stunning potential. All beauty was hijacked from within. Enticed by revenge, this man robbed others of life. And for murder he has paid the ultimate price. His execution was the most bloody and gruesome demise ever devised by human hand.

Struck by her heartbreak, Ruach hovers motionless over a valley between two hills. On one side is the execution site. On the other: Jerusalem, the city Ruach once called home; a city once overflowing with peace and prosperity, freedom and equality.

Today, fear fills Jerusalem. Nehemiah's reforms of four centuries ago are no more than a fleeting, distant, tantalising memory. Now all in Jerusalem must bow to the most powerful dominion of all: the Roman Empire.

All must declare 'Caesar is Lord.'

And acknowledge Herod as King.

Or face the ultimate retribution: crucifixion.

Each drip of blood from a crucified rebel communicates a chilling political message: put a foot out of line, dare to disrupt the peace, dare to challenge the Empire's authority, and this is how you shall spend your final hours.

You shall die as a disgraced public spectacle.

You shall die as an outcast, tied to a disfigured tree outside the city walls.

For Jews in Jerusalem the punishment is particularly poignant: according to Moses, '*anyone who is hung on a tree is under God's curse.*'[1]

Our fist thumps the Phase Five wall in petulant frustration. 'How long must this curse go on?' we scream helplessly.

'Where are you, Yahweh?

'What has happened to Rescue?

'What has happened to your love?'

Our jarring words hang in the silence, tangled in tight choked air. Our chest contracts, as if battling an acute hunger.

'People will wander through the land troubled and hungry.'
The silence broken, our back clicks rigid.
'They will look up and curse their king and their God. They will look around them at their land and see only trouble, darkness and awful gloom.'[2]

Though we have no sense of where it comes from, this voice sounds real and honest. It seems to connect with our pain.

'But suddenly there will be no more gloom for the land that suffered.'[3]

As if pulled by the rising tones of optimism even the air seems to loosen and our eyes focus once more on the Headquarters wall. To our great surprise the next words we read are those just heard. Writing seven centuries before Jerusalem's Roman occupation, Isaiah elaborates:

'A child has been born to us; God has given a son to us...
His name will be Wonderful Counsellor,
Powerful God,
Father Who Lives For Ever,
Prince of Peace.
Power and peace will be in his kingdom...
He will rule as king on David's throne.'[4]

Scepticism explodes within us: some of these credentials are just nonsense. How could a father live forever?! Worse still, how could a human be 'Powerful God'?! Isn't this the most outrageous blasphemy?

With a stroppy child-like swing of the arm we rip the passage down from the wall. Further narrative lies beneath.

A waft of farmyard faeces fills the air as a teenage mother rests in the arms of her fiancé. Exhausted but elated, Mary sits captivated by the tiny rhythmic breaths of her newborn son.

So beautiful and tender.

So precious and fragile.

So helpless and innocent.

Could it really be true? Could this miniature bundle of joy really be Israel's long-awaited great warrior?

Israel's Messiah?

A liberator like Moses?

A leader like David, reigning over a universal kingdom of peace?

The Roman Empire may already claim to be a universal kingdom of peace, but it is peace by coercion, peace by fear. Extortionate taxes keep the rich in power and the poor in poverty. To reinforce his authority, Emperor Augustus even describes himself as 'the son of the gods'. All over the Empire, temples are being built to worship Augustus as a god on earth.

A god in human flesh.

For Mary this is the most outrageous blasphemy, the ultimate denial of Yahweh; the utmost reason why her newborn son simply has to fulfil his liberation mission, and *rule over the people of Jacob forever*.[5]

Forever.

Mary's son will truly, literally, rule forever - because *nothing is impossible with God*.[6] Mary knows it is true because nine months ago, she conceived - despite never having had sex.

And ever since Isaiah wrote about a young mother naming her child *'Immanuel'*[7] - meaning 'God with us' - a virgin becoming pregnant has been a much anticipated, highly significant sign. The miracle child would be the sign that God's favour had returned. The curse would be over. God would be for us, with us, once again.

Mary leans down and kisses her Immanuel's forehead, overwhelmed by the knowledge that her miraculous conception was caused by the life-bringing breath of Ruach. Which means, the child in her arms, truly, literally is 'God with us.'

The child she kisses, truly, literally is *'the Son of God.'*[8]

Mary is holding Yahweh in human flesh.

1.	Deuteronomy 21:23	5.	Luke 1:33
2.	Isaiah 8:21-22	6.	Luke 1:37
3.	Isaiah 9:1	7.	Isaiah 7:14
4.	Isaiah 9:6-7	8.	Luke 1:35

5.02 - Jesus the Great

Four hundred years ago in Babylon the Messiah arrived.

The Messiah liberated the exiles.

Or so they thought.

Hailed as Yahweh's *'appointed king,'* Cyrus the Great, the King of Persia, swept in from the east, winning battle after battle. *'He is my shepherd,'* Yahweh said of Cyrus. *'He will say to Jerusalem, "You will be built again!"'*[1]

And he did.

Cyrus set the exiles free.

His tolerance was unprecedented.

His timing accurately fulfilled Jeremiah's seventy years of exile prophecy.[2]

Yet as the years passed, doubts rose over Cyrus' Messiah credentials. The prophet Ezekiel had foreseen the exiles returning to paradise. But in reality, Jerusalem remained ravaged and derelict.

So perhaps Zerubbabel - a direct descendant of David - had been the true Messiah for rebuilding Jerusalem's Temple.

Or perhaps Nehemiah was the Messiah for administering justice, freedom and equality: all prominent features in Ezekiel's paradise.[3]

Or perhaps the Messiah would be Alexander the Great, a mighty warrior overthrowing Persian power wherever he pleased. The Judeans surrendered willingly to Alexander's revolution and sure enough, the prolific killer spared their blood. Even Egypt welcomed Alexander as their great liberator, honouring him as Pharaoh, exalting him as a son of the gods.

A god in human flesh.

Alexander was revered for ushering in a whole new world: a Greek world more enlightened and developed; a world built upon the teachings of Pythagoras, Plato and Aristotle. However, for Jews trying to live in careful adherence to Yahweh's laws, the new world posed problems. An athletics stadium built in Jerusalem not only forced participants to compete naked - embarrassing enough for circumcised Jews - but each sporting spectacle was dedicated to Zeus, King of the Greek gods.

Uncomfortable cultural compromises continued.

Until Judah's Greek King made the situation untenable.

Antiochus outlawed all practices honouring Yahweh.

And enforced the worship of Zeus.

Antiochus even declared himself as the visible manifestation of Zeus.

A god in human flesh.

Failure to submit was punishable by death.

Now more than ever the Judeans needed their Messiah, their own 'Great' warrior like Cyrus or Alexander.

Step forward Judas Maccabeus. With an ill-equipped

band of amateurs, Judas tore into Antiochus' army, destroying all traces of Zeus, liberating Jerusalem from Greek rule. Over the next eighty years the politically independent Maccabean dynasty stretched out its borders and Ezekiel's vision of a restored Israel,[4] as large as that ruled by King David, edged ever closer.

Judas Maccabeus was the Messiah. Wasn't he?

When Roman General Pompey stormed into Jerusalem, claiming it for the new world superpower, he marched into the Temple's Holy of Holies and revealed a truly shocking secret. In Ezekiel's vision, Yahweh cheered, '*I will live here among the Israelites forever*';[5] the city will be known as, "Yahweh *Is There*."'[6] But inside the exclusive room famously housing the Shekinah of Yahweh, Pompey found nothing.

No swirling cloud.

No tangible presence.

Yahweh was not there.

The Shekinah had not returned to her Temple.

Ezekiel's paradise had clearly not arrived yet.

Confused and bewildered, Jewish scholars started to pour over the prophecies from their past. They discovered that Daniel had added to Jeremiah's seventy years of exile by describing a further period of four hundred and ninety years before '*the appointed leader comes.*'[7] During that time, Daniel had foreseen the rise and fall of three further kingdoms[8] before one final kingdom, the Kingdom of God, crushed *all the other kingdoms* and continued *forever*.[9]

So far, history has proved Daniel right.

First Cyrus the Great inaugurated the Persian Kingdom.

Then Alexander the Great brought the world of the Greeks.

Now Herod the Great rules within the Empire of Rome.

And Daniel's four hundred and ninety years are nearly up.

Having slain challenger after challenger to earn his powerful position, King Herod is on full alert. Not content with simply presenting himself as the Judeans' Messiah - calling himself 'The King of the Jews' and reconstructing Jerusalem's Temple - Herod is anxious to eliminate the true Messiah before it is too late. So when reports reach Herod that the Messiah may have been born in Bethlehem, he does not hesitate: Herod orders the death of all *baby boys in Bethlehem*.[10]

Thirty years later, Jesus sits by a well sweltering in the midday sun, when a woman approaches to draw water.

'Whoever drinks the water I give will never be thirsty again,' Jesus says to the woman. *'The water I give will become a spring of water flowing up inside that person, giving eternal life.'*[11]

Taken aback, the woman pauses, not knowing how to reply. In Ezekiel's paradise, a river flowed out from the Temple, filled with everlasting water. By referencing Ezekiel's living water - fresh, invigorating, teeming with life[12] - this arrogant stranger has touched upon her nation's deepest aches and pains, hopes and expectations; a topic clouded with confusion and rumour, claims and counter-claims.

'I know that the Messiah is coming,' the woman replies. *'When the Messiah comes he will explain everything.'*[13]

With the smile of someone divulging a long-kept secret, Jesus looks straight into the woman's eyes and reveals, *'I am he - I, the one talking to you.'*[14]

The Kingdom of God - Ezekiel's paradise - has arrived. The revolution of Jesus the Great is about to begin.

1. Isaiah 44:28
2. Jeremiah 29:10
3. Ezekiel 45:9-10
4. Ezekiel 48:1-8
5. Ezekiel 43:7
6. Ezekiel 48:35
7. Daniel 9:25
8. Daniel 2:39-40
9. Daniel 2:44
10. Matthew 2:16
11. John 4:13
12. Ezekiel 47:8-9
13. John 4:25
14. John 4:26

5.03 – The Pivotal Moment

A grin flickers across our face; our eyes are alight in wonder. The words of Ezekiel's vision have reached down through the centuries and seeped into the consciousness of Jesus' world. What's more, here beneath our feet, buried amongst the debris of our fall from the loft, there are potentially hundreds of similar Phase Four texts.

Each could shape our understanding of Phase Five. Each could reveal Jesus' motivations and ambitions; illuminate his actions and achievements.

So with renewed vigour we fall down to our knees and start to sieve through the Phase Four wreckage. We uncover the occasional undamaged gem; even an entire scroll. But the majority of the texts are tattered and torn; scattered fragments which need piecing together.

Before long we have made our first connection.

'I became very angry and hid from you for a time, but I will show you mercy with kindness forever.'

Our head shakes in bewilderment as we read the words of Isaiah again.

'This day is like the time of Noah to me. I promised then that I would never flood the world again. In the same way, I promise I will not be angry with you or punish again.'[1]

Really?

Our journey so far has taught us that God is Love.

And Love demands justice.

And justice demands punishment.

Is there really a day coming when Yahweh's anger and punishments will be no more?

But the second text in our hand is clear. Yahweh told Jeremiah, *'I will make an everlasting covenant with them: I will never stop doing good to them.'*[2]

This shakes us to the very core of our being.

This shakes our view of God: it shakes our fear.

'I will enjoy doing good to them. And with my whole being I will surely plant them in this land and make them grow.'[3]

Our heart flutters and skips. There is a day coming when Yahweh's goodness will be everlasting; covenanted, contracted, for all time. Somehow - and we have no idea how - there is a moment coming, a pivotal moment, when the God of Love and Justice ceases to dispense punishments. And from that moment on, only goodness will remain.

We spring back to our feet. Perhaps Jesus is going to bring about this pivotal moment?

From a young age, Jesus has stood out as a prodigy of the texts. Aged just twelve, his wisdom and insights impressed even the most knowledgeable scholars in Jerusalem.[4] And in today's Jewish world, that elevates Jesus to a vitally important position. Communities gather weekly, knowing that a correct interpretation and faithful application of Yahweh's Laws can mean the difference between life and death.

In recent months, Jesus has been out on the road, teaching in synagogue after synagogue.

Today, the prodigy has returned home.

There is a noisy hubbub as Jesus stands up from his seat and collects the scroll of Isaiah. 'Do you remember when…' friends whisper to each other, recalling fond memories from Jesus' childhood.

Jesus looks up. He is ready. He has found his page. *'The Spirit of the Lord is on me, because he has anointed me to proclaim good news to the poor. He has sent me to proclaim freedom for the prisoners and recovery of sight for the blind.'*[5]

We instantly recognise the words. They were on the scroll we found, the one that survived our fall intact.

Inside is stanza after stanza of romantic poetry:

'Because I love Jerusalem,' one portion begins.

  'You will never again be called the People that God Left,
Nor your land the Land that God Destroyed.

  You will be called the People God Loves,
  And your land will be called the Bride of God…
As a man rejoices over his new wife,
  So your God will rejoice over you.'[6]

Once again the language is absolute: Jerusalem will never again be destroyed. Yahweh's punishments will be no more. Only Yahweh's goodness, Yahweh's gentle restoration, only Yahweh's love and celebration will remain.

This is the pivotal moment described again.

As we read on, the long-term aspirations expand far beyond the restoration of one city. *'Look, I will make new heavens and a new earth,'*[7] Yahweh says.

There will be no more crying.

No more pain.

No more injustice.

No more bloodshed.

A person who lives one hundred years will be called young.[8]

Even animals will live in harmony.[9]

'Like babies you will be nursed and held in my arms and bounced on my knees,' the tender romantic promises. *'I will comfort you as a mother comforts her child.'*[10]

This will be the age of everlasting kindness.

This is the age that every Jew is waiting for, hoping for, longing for.

And this is the text that Jesus has chosen to read in the synagogue.

'God sent me,' Jesus continues, *'to free those who have been treated unfairly, and to announce the time when the Lord will show his kindness.'*[11]

Absolute silence.

All are struck by a thought of cataclysmic proportions.

When Jesus just said, 'God sent me,' was he saying…?

Was he… is he saying that the time of kindness is actually here? Now?

A smile stretches across Jesus' cheeks.

'While you heard these words just now,' his words build to a momentous crescendo: *'they were coming true!'*[12]

1. Isaiah 54:8-9
2. Jeremiah 32:40 (NIV)
3. Jeremiah 32:41
4. Luke 2:47
5. Luke 4:18 (NIV)
6. Isaiah 62:1-5
7. Isaiah 65:17
8. Isaiah 65:20
9. Isaiah 65:25
10. Isaiah 66:12-13
11. Luke 4:19
12. Luke 4:21

5.04 – A New Israel

His flesh shrivelled like rotting fruit, Jesus staggers and falls into a field of lush green grass. To our astonishment - for forty days - Jesus has been living with nothing to eat or drink in blistering desert, pushing his body to its limits in an inhospitable wilderness, exposing himself to mental agony and torment.

As we picture Jesus recovering, lying out on the grass, stretching his tongue to lick rain drops from a leaf, we wonder why? Why would Jesus torture himself like that? To mentally prepare for the challenges ahead? To train his body for combat? Or was it a symbolic act, sending a message to the masses?

Forty days is not an arbitrary number. Forty is significant, not least because Israel had to wait forty years in the desert before entering the Promised Land.

Dots start to join in our mind.

As we look back over the beginnings of Phase Five, we notice further connections between Jesus' life and the history of Israel. To begin with, Jesus was born in Bethlehem, the home of David. Then King Herod ordered the massacre of all baby boys in Bethlehem,[1] like the Egyptian Pharaoh at the beginning of Phase Three. Moses' mother saved her newborn from Pharaoh's butchery, and likewise Jesus' parents fled with their precious child to Egypt.

Where they stayed until Herod died.

Which means, Jesus came out of Egypt.[2]

Just like Israel.

Then there's the list of men who form the central hub of Jesus' growing army. Jesus has chosen twelve closest supporters to deliberately echo the twelve tribes of Israel - hasn't he?

The evidence appears compelling: whether consciously or subconsciously, Jesus' life so far is retelling Israel's story. But to what extent, we wonder? Will Jesus continue to re-enact the story precisely as it happened, warts and all? Will his life include a Babylonian exile? Or will Jesus tell the story how it was supposed to happen? Will Jesus 'choose life'?

Suddenly a voice stuns us still.

'Your mother was like a vine… the vine had many branches and gave much fruit.'

The voice is not from above or below us, behind or in front. It just seems to surround us; cut right through us.

'But the vine was pulled up by its roots in anger and thrown to the ground.[3] I planted you as a special vine, as a very good seed. How then did you turn into a wild vine that grows bad fruit?'[4]

The voice is devastated, distraught, as if grieving the loss of a loved one.

'This is a funeral song.[5] What more could I have done for my vineyard? … I expected good grapes to grow, why were there only bad ones?'[6]

The voice chokes as if tears have dripped into the

mourner's mouth. We are moved by the words, moved by the emotion, but we do not know why. We do not understand why anyone would be singing a funeral song over the loss of some grapes.

Our eyes sweep over the Phase Five wall, searching for references to grapes or vines. Sure enough, up in the top right-hand corner, in large letters, Jesus says, '*I am the true vine.*'[7]

Our initial rush of success quickly succumbs to confusion. The answer has only opened up more questions: if Jesus is the vine, does this mean that Jesus went sour? Is Jesus the one that the voice is mourning? The quote is attached to the wall along a folded hinge. Underneath the flap, Isaiah explains, '*The vineyard belonging to* Yahweh *is the nation of Israel; the garden that he loves is the people of Judah. He looked for justice, but there was only killing. He hoped for right living, but there were only cries of pain.*'[8]

Israel was the vine that went sour, not Jesus. So when Jesus describes himself as 'the true vine' he is identifying himself as a new Israel, a true Israel, the embodiment of everything that Israel was originally meant to be. He will be the justice that Yahweh has always sought, the right living that was craved.

To the left of the vine revelation, another hinged card catches our attention. In a vivid, royal blue font, Jesus says, '*I am the good shepherd.*'[9]

What does he mean this time?

We lift the flap and peer beneath.

A passage by Ezekiel describes how Israel's Phase

Four exile was brought about by a catalogue of incompetent, self-indulgent leaders. *'The sheep were scattered, because there was no shepherd, and they became food for every wild animal.'*[10] Then a highlighted line signals a shift in the account. Yahweh says: *'I myself, will search for my sheep and take care of them.'*[11] Yahweh will round up his scattered sheep. Yahweh will be Israel's one true, good shepherd and will lead his flock home to abundant idyllic pastures.

'I will make a covenant of peace with them,' says the good shepherd, *'and rid the land of wild beasts.'*[12]

At the end of Phase Four, the lost sheep were rounded up and brought home to Jerusalem. But there can be no idyllic pastures, no paradise and peace - no Promised Land - while the Romans rule.

Jesus must rid the land of its wild beasts.

The Messiah must destroy the formidable Romans.

1. Matthew 2:16
2. Matthew 2:15
3. Ezekiel 19:10-12
4. Jeremiah 2:21
5. Ezekiel 19:14
6. Isaiah 5:4
7. John 15:1
8. Isaiah 5:7
9. John 10:11
10. Ezekiel 34:5-6
11. Ezekiel 34:11
12. Ezekiel 34:25 (NIV)

5.05 – Invincible

Peter knows how it works by now. All James has to do is throw out some brash, absolute statement and his younger brother John takes the bait. No matter how obvious it is that John is right, James never backs down; he enjoys winding his brother up too much.

At the best of times the immature tussles test Peter's patience. But today it is cold and overcast, and they are sitting on a jagged rock high up a mountain; if Jesus wasn't off praying in the distance, Peter would have wrung their necks long ago.

'We should never have abandoned our father's business. At least fishing gave us a secure future.' James flings his arm out in the direction of Jesus. 'This madman could get us killed.'

'We made our decision and we stick to it. No-one would turn down a chance to follow a rabbi like this.'

'But is he even a rabbi, John? No true rabbi would have us as disciples. We're uneducated, unqualified. We've been taken in by a rogue, a showman, a wannabe. I mean, what rabbi ever calls God, "Abba"? They don't even call God...' James lowers his voice, '"Yahweh" anymore.'

John shoots his brother a disapproving glare. 'James, you've seen what he's done. I've lost count of the people he's healed. And you know that he uses no tricks. This man is like Moses or Elijah. They both spoke intimately with God up Mount Sinai[1] and that's what Jesus is doing now. He calls God "Abba" because they have a close relationship.'

'It's all part of the act, John; just another of his outrageous claims. You heard Jesus when he said, *"Moses wrote about me"*[2] and that he had come to fulfil all of Moses' laws.[3] It's ridiculous, impossible. This man is arrogant, obnoxious, out of his mind.'

'No, James. You're the one who's obnoxious. Jesus is the most intelligent man you've ever met. He summarised Moses' entire law in just one sentence: *"Do to others what you want them to do to you."*[4] Only a truly exceptional man could have managed such a feat. His teaching emphasised our motives, our attitudes, our thoughts, our heart.[5] And when he was teaching the crowds on that mountain, you've got to admit that he looked a bit like Moses.'

'What about when he said he was *"greater than Solomon"*?[6] Or when he claimed he was *"greater than the Temple"*?[7] That's not intelligent, that's just...'

In one swift motion, Peter is bearing down on James, pressing his finger into James' cheek and up into his eye. Through gritted teeth he yells, 'He is the Messiah,[8] you idiot! Why can't you see that? *Even the winds and waves obey him!*[9] We were going to die in that storm and all Jesus said was, *"Quiet! Be still!"*[10] and the waves cowered in retreat. He made me walk on water. He is *the Son of God.*'[11]

James dare not speak.

'Lay off him Peter. You can't know for sure that Jesus is

the Messiah.'

Peter looks round, eyes blazing, staggered by John's defence of his brother.

'Having power over sea doesn't make Jesus the Messiah. It just makes him like Moses; or like Elijah and Elisha, parting the Jordan River.'[12]

Peter pulls back his finger from James' eye. His shoulders slump in exasperation. 'But Jesus is better than Moses, Elijah and Elisha. Elisha fed one hundred people with twenty loaves and a sack of grain, and there was some *food left over*.[13] Well, Jesus fed thousands with just five loaves and two fish, and we *filled twelve baskets with* the leftovers.[14] Elijah and Elisha both revived one dead child[15] but Jesus has brought back two.'[16]

'But Peter, Jesus can't be the Messiah because *Elijah must come first*.[17] Malachi said that Elijah would return before the *"great and terrible day of* judgement",[18] when *"the proud and evil* become *like straw"*, when the Romans *"burn like a hot furnace."*'[19]

A blazing fireball explodes.

Peering through shielded eyes, the trio see Jesus' *face* shining *bright like the sun, his clothes* a vehement *white*.[20] Two mysterious men stand beside Jesus, talking to him. Then a voice booms across the sky, *'This is my Son, whom I love, and I am very pleased with him.'*[21]

Peter, James and John fall flat to the ground.

They do not know how long it is.

Until an arm ushers them up.

'You're ok.'

Jesus' smile is warm.

The lights have gone; so too have his companions.

Jesus helps Peter, James and John to their feet and as they start to walk down the mountain Jesus reveals that he had been talking with Moses and Elijah. And for the next hour, John does not hear another word Jesus says.

Because Elijah!

Elijah!

Elijah has returned.

The day of judgement is imminent.

Jesus is greater than Elijah, and Elijah never died - he was *taken up to heaven in a whirlwind*[22] - which means not even the mighty Romans will be able to withstand Jesus' onslaught.

Jesus will be unstoppable.

Indestructible.

Invincible.

The blood that Jesus spills will liberate the world.

1. 1 Kings 19:13
2. John 5:46
3. Matthew 5:17
4. Matthew 7:12
5. Matthew 5:21-48
6. Matthew 12:42
7. Matthew 12:6
8. Matthew 16:16
9. Mark 4:41
10. Mark 4:39
11. Matthew 14:33
12. 2 Kings 2:8 & 2:13
13. 2 Kings 4:44
14. Matthew 14:20
15. 1 Kings 17:22 & 4:37
16. Luke 7:14 & 8:54
17. Matthew 17:10
18. Malachi 4:5
19. Malachi 4:1
20. Matthew 17:2
21. Matthew 17:5
22. 2 Kings 2:11

5.06 – Anointed

It is nearly ten years since smooth golden oil poured over Caiaphas' head and raced down his robes. Anointed as high priest of Jerusalem, appointed with Rome's full approval, on that day Caiaphas had felt ready for anything. All he had to do was keep the peace in Jerusalem and Rome's blessing was assured.

Over the decade, potential uprisings have come and gone, quelled with relative ease. But there's something different about Jesus' threat. Down every street swords are being sharpened, ready for revolution.

Caiaphas must decide urgently whether to endorse Jesus - and face the wrath of Rome - or stop him before it is too late.

'If Jesus continues to do these things, the Romans will crush us. They will *take away our Temple and our nation*.[1] They could wipe out Israel in a day. God's chosen people: gone forever.'

Caiaphas sits forlorn as advice flies at him from every angle.

'We asked Jesus straight out, "*If you are the Christ tell us plainly.*"[2] The true Messiah would never hide his identity. But do you know what Jesus said? "*The father and I are one*"!'[3]

'What kind of answer is that? Tell me, where did he study?'

'He says that his teaching "*comes from God.*"[4] He said, "*I was sent by the One who is true.*"'[5]

'It's just sheer arrogance.'

'It's lunacy.'

'His lies are dangerous. He just says what people want to hear. Jesus even claimed, *"whoever obeys my teaching will never die."*[6]

'Thankfully the crowds didn't just swallow that one. *"Even Abraham and the prophets died,"* they shouted. *"Do you think that you are greater than our father Abraham?"*[7]

'You won't believe Jesus' reply. He answered, *"Abraham was very happy that he would see my day."*[8]

The council erupts in derision.

Caiaphas signals for quiet.

'Who can testify that Jesus said this?'

More than half the room raises their hand.

'But sir, there is more. When the crowds howled, *"You have never seen Abraham! You are not even 50 years old"* Jesus' response was so abhorrent, well, I can't even repeat it.'

'You have to. I have to know.'

'You won't like it. It's blasphemy. He said, *"I tell you the truth, before Abraham was even born, I am!"*[9]

Caiaphas bows his head.

He has heard enough.

Anyone who blasphemes the name of the LORD must be put to death.[10]

Our hands trace through our hair and slide down over our face. Jesus is telling the truth and yet we cannot blame the priests for reacting as they have. By saying, 'Before Abraham was born, I am,' Jesus is implying that he is thousands of years old. Who would honestly believe that?

The curious phrase rocks about in our mind. Why would Jesus say it like that? Why not say, 'I was alive before Abraham'? Why say, 'I am'?

I am.

I am.

I am that I am.

Our fingers click as we realise it. 'I am' is a direct reference to the name 'Yahweh.' That is why it is so blasphemous. Jesus said 'I am' to deliberately connect himself with Yahweh.

Our muscles relax.

Back in Phase Three, Moses' Egyptian liberation had seemed impossible.

But with Yahweh it was possible.

And Jesus is Yahweh in human flesh.

His victory is guaranteed.

Because Jesus is all-powerful.

Invincible.

Jesus cannot die.

Mary's heart pounds as she looks into Jesus' eyes and strokes his rugged hair. This is the greatest man she will ever know. He is kind and compassionate, honest and open. When her brother Lazarus died, Mary saw the tears streaming down Jesus' face.[11]

Mary looks across at Lazarus laughing, sharing a joke with Jesus' disciples. The precious sight leaves Mary in no doubt: Jesus has brought life to the dead; he is *'the resurrection and the life';*[12] these are the last days of the old world, the final days before the dead return to life.[13]

Jesus is the Messiah.

And yet Mary looks into Jesus' eyes and she cannot help but fear for his life. This man that she loves so dearly: he is no great warrior.

He is strong and confident, brave and assured.

But he is no fighter; Jesus lacks a warrior spirit.

King David was Israel's greatest warrior, winning battle after battle, expanding Israel's borders, liberating from enemies all around. But David never fought in his own strength. It was the anointing breath of Ruach who gave David his success. When he was just a boy, smooth golden oil was poured over his head and *from that day on,* God's *Spirit worked in David.*[14]

Jesus needs dousing in the same warrior spirit.

Because 'Messiah' literally means 'the anointed one.'

Mary lifts up a bottle of her finest perfume and pours the rich aromatic oil over Jesus' head. The crowded room falls unerringly silent. Jesus closes his eyes as the liquid flows over his body and down to his feet. Next Mary loosens her hair down to her waist and wipes back and forth, massaging and drying Jesus' feet.

Shock turns to outrage.

Frantic protests fly.

Wiping the oil from his eyes, Jesus stands to his feet. He looks around the room, catching every eye; then announces, *'It was right for* Mary *to save this perfume for today, the day for me to be prepared for burial.'*[15]

1. John 11:48
2. John 10:24
3. John 10:30
4. John 17:7
5. John 7:28
6. John 8:51
7. John 8:53-54
8. John 8:56
9. John 8:57-58
10. Leviticus 24:16 (NIV)
11. John 11:35
12. John 11:25
13. John 11:24
14. 1 Samuel 16:13
15. John 12:7

5.07 – How The Tables Have Turned

Judas Iscariot lies on his back, staring out at the stars, marvelling at the world in which he lives. When dawn breaks, he will be fighting in the war to end all wars, fighting for the new Jerusalem promised by the prophets; a Jerusalem free from oppression and injustice, filled with peace and prosperity; a Jerusalem that the God of Abraham will be proud to call home.

With one hand fixed to the hilt of his sword, Judas mentally rehearses each swing of his weapon. Picking out a light in the sky, he tries to focus his mind.

'It was right for Mary to save this perfume for today, the day for me to be prepared for burial.'

Judas screws his eyes: just when he is fully focused on the battle ahead, these words come back to haunt him. What did Jesus mean? Was he conceding defeat? Is Jesus expecting to die in this war?!

Judas shakes his head, trying to throw the thought from his mind. In its place, another terrifying image takes over: the sight of Jesus, only yesterday, breaking down in a flood of tears.

Why, Jesus, why?

This was a humiliating public display of weakness.

This was not Messiah.

'You did not recognise the time when God came to save you,'[1] Jesus exclaimed as he wept. But Judas cannot understand it. When Jesus rode toward Jerusalem,

awkwardly and ungainly on a young donkey, it was only the religious leaders who had wanted to stop him. Which was hardly surprising since they are puppets of Rome; the system works for them. But the vast majority had recognised Jesus' deliberate enactment of Zechariah's well-known Messianic prophecy:

'Shout for joy, people of Jerusalem!

   Your king is coming for you.

He does what is right, and he saves.

   He is gentle and riding on a donkey.'[2]

With Passover just days away, Jesus' timing was impeccable. Israel's new liberator had announced his arrival when the city was awash with pilgrims, flocking to Jerusalem to celebrate Moses' remarkable rescue. The cosmopolitan crowds cheered at the top of their voices: 'God bless the kingdom of our father David! That kingdom is coming!'[3]

Judas grins, his finger resting on the tip of his blade.

When dawn breaks, Judas will fight for Jesus' revolution.

And he will fight to stay alive.

With fire in his eyes, Jesus strides menacingly, looking every bit a warrior. Eyes fixed firmly upon his target, he storms into the Temple courtyard and crashes into the traders, overturning their tables, sending merchandise sprawling. 'My Temple will be called a house of prayer,' Jesus bellows. 'But you are changing it into a "hideout for robbers."'[4]

For his opening strike, Jesus has targeted Rome's

commercial corruption of Jerusalem's most sacred venue.

With the merchants scarpering, Jesus ushers into the courtyard those previously prohibited from entering. And for the rest of the day, Jesus cares for society's outcasts, healing the blind and the crippled.[5]

Judas allows himself a smile. Now this is Messiah: fierce and uncompromising, restoring David's Temple, confronting corruption, fighting injustice, bringing dignity, equality, new life and health.

Young children dance with abandon in the courtyard, chanting over and over, '*Praise to the son of David.*'[6]

This is Messiah: and even energetic kids can see it.

The following day, Jesus heads straight inside the Temple and starts to teach. At first, Judas interprets this as one final rallying cry, one final attempt to get the religious leaders on side. But as the day wears on, to Judas' horror, Jesus becomes locked in furious theological debate.

Jesus ducks and dives, avoiding theological traps.

He debates the payment of taxes.

He defends the resurrection of the dead.

He discusses the greatest commandment.[7]

But all the time Jesus is on the defensive, and gaining precious little ground.

Judas' patience is waning. Why can't Jesus see that these fractious debates could go on for weeks? Can't Jesus see that he is missing his moment, wasting the wave of optimism and support?

Suddenly there's silence.

A lengthy, deathly pause.[8]

Before Jesus launches a blistering offensive.

'You *blind fools...*[9] *You are snakes!*'[10] Savage and scathing, Jesus places punch after punch on his opponents. '*You are full of hypocrisy and evil.*[11] You are a *child of hell.*'[12] Exiting in a thunderous cloud of fury, Jesus roars, '*Do you see all these great buildings? Not one stone will be left on another. Every stone will be thrown to the ground.*'[13]

His supporters stand stunned. Only Peter, James, John and Andrew dare follow their predatory master.

When the four return a few hours later, they share Jesus' grave expression.

'"*Great trouble will come upon this land,*"' Peter explains, relaying Jesus' words, '"*and God will be angry with these people. They will be killed by the sword and taken as prisoners to all nations. Jerusalem will be crushed.*"'[14]

Judas stares out in disbelief at the stars in the night sky; how the tables have turned.

This is not Messiah. This is the opposite of Messiah.

This is judgment, not liberation.

This is Jeremiah, not Moses.

But there's more: Jesus says his followers will be hunted down, arrested and killed.[15]

Fighting back the tears, Judas drops his sword to the ground.

He sees no other way out.

He must turn against Jesus.

It is the only way to stay alive.

1. Luke 19:44
2. Zechariah 9:9
3. Mark 11:10
4. Matthew 21:13
5. Matthew 21:14
6. Matthew 21:15
7. Matthew 22:15-40
8. Matthew 22:46
9. Matthew 23:19
10. Matthew 23:33
11. Matthew 23:28
12. Matthew 23:15 (NIV)
13. Mark 13:2
14. Luke 21:24
15. Matthew 24:9

5.08 – Invitation to Feast

There is not a soul around.

Not a sound.

Just a light breeze brushes Jesus' hair as he strides through the darkness of night, climbing high into the mountains.

Feeling for the cragged edges of his favourite spot, Jesus takes his seat, closes his eyes and breathes in slowly, before exhaling deeply. He is weary, burdened down by the busyness, the crowds, each individual with such great needs.

Arms wrap around Jesus' shoulders, squeezing him tight. He opens his eyes to see Abba sitting beside him.

'I am so proud of you my Son. I love you with all of my heart.'

Ruach rushes around their embrace. She dances through Jesus' tired body, breathing into his lungs. 'Keep going my love,' she whispers delicately. 'We are with you.'

Abba looks deeply into Yeshua's eyes. He can see the strain, the heaviness, the heartbreak.

'Look around you, Yeshua. We told Isaiah that we would *prepare a feast on this mountain for all people,* promising the finest food and wine. Isaiah declared that *on this mountain* we *will destroy the veil that covers all nations.* Oh, Yeshua, we *will destroy death forever* and *wipe every tear from every face.'*[1]

'Everyone, absolutely everyone, is invited to our feast,' adds Ruach, bristling with delight.

'All people, all nations.'

'Even Roman soldiers.'

Jesus smiles at Ruach's playfulness. He recalls the Roman general who begged him to heal his bedridden servant. Jesus welcomed him. Jesus praised him. Jesus turned to his flabbergasted followers and declared, *'This is the greatest faith I have found, even in Israel. Many people will come from the east and from the west and will sit and eat with Abraham, Isaac and Jacob in the kingdom of heaven.'*[2]

Everyone is invited to the feast.

People from all over the world will choose to attend.

'The kingdom of heaven,' says Abba, *'is like a king who prepared a wedding feast for his son.*[3] *The king said to his servants... "Go to the street corners and invite everyone you can find to come to my feast."'*[4]

'Invite everyone,' repeats Ruach, grinning.

Jesus lets her words soothe his heart.

'But the Israelites rejected their invites.[5] They abandoned their mandate to invite others to our feast.'

'Now my darling, you are proclaiming Love's great marriage proposal. You are on earth, down on one knee, inviting the world into intimacy.'

'And those who say "yes" will feast at Heaven's romantic wedding.'

'They shall sit at the top table, centre of attention.'

'They shall sit as our newly ordained Bride.'

'The sumptuously beautiful Bride of Love.'

Ruach swirls around Abba, and overflowing in perfect love and affection, together the Lovers of Elohim ache in eager expectation, waiting and longing for the day they marry their one true love.

Jesus sits mesmerised. His heart is ablaze, overwhelmed by the promise of a perfect, love-drenched wedding; overcome by the prospect of his Bride gliding gracefully down the aisle towards him.

He recalls his first miracle, at a wedding, turning six hundred litres of water into sensational wine.[6]

He recalls turning five loaves into a feast for thousands on a Galilean hillside.

An abundance of bread.

An abundance of wine.

These were tastes of the future feast foreseen by Isaiah.

They were extravagant announcements: *'The Kingdom of Heaven is near.'*[7]

They were Jesus down on one knee, his heart poured out, awaiting response.

With sunlight flickering off the mountaintops and birdsong welcoming the dawn, Abba and Ruach help Jesus to his feet and watch him step forward with clear determination.

Today is Passover, the annual commemoration of Moses' Egyptian liberation. Throughout his childhood, Jesus' parents would take him to Jerusalem's joyous festivities,[8] and each year the celebrations would thrill his heart. But this year…

This year, Jesus and his closest followers will be locked

away in an inconspicuous room.

Amid high tensions, the room will be sombre.

Suspicious.

Wary and apprehensive.

Clambering down the mountain, knowing that this will be his last *Passover meal until it is given its true meaning in the kingdom of God,*[9] Jesus rehearses his movements. He plans to initiate a whole new Passover feast, a whole new way to celebrate liberation. He will fill a cup to the brim with wine, lift it into the air and say, *'When you drink this, do it to remember me.'*[10] He will break bread, pass it round the table and say, 'Eat *this in remembrance of me.'*[11]

An abundance of bread.

An abundance of wine.

For future friends and followers of Jesus this is their regular invitation to feast. Engaged for marriage, his future Bride shall dine on bread and wine.

She shall remember.

Celebrate.

And ache in eager expectation, waiting and longing for the day she marries her one true Love.

1. Isaiah 25:6–8
2. Matthew 8:11
3. Matthew 22:2
4. Matthew 22:8–9
5. Matthew 22:3
6. John 2:11
7. Matthew 4:17
8. Luke 2:41
9. Luke 22:16
10. 1 Corinthians 11:25
11. Luke 22:19 (NIV)

5.09 – There Will Be Blood

Positioned beside the narrative of Jesus serving bread and wine, we are intrigued by a page of poetry taped to the wall along its top edge only:

'*I am Israel's father,*'[1] declares Yahweh.

'*Israel is my dear son,*

The child that I love.

Yes, I often speak against Israel,

But I still remember him.

I love him very much

And I want to comfort him.'[2]

Incredibly, these tender words of affection were spoken in the context of Jerusalem's Babylonian destruction.

'*Look, the time is coming,*' declares Yahweh, '*when I will make a new covenant.*'[3]

The words leap out from the page: new covenant!

Without Yahweh's covenants, the Rescue Mission would be nowhere. Each has pulled us forward, closer to the restoration of paradise.

'The new covenant *will not be like the agreement I made with their ancestors when I took them out of Egypt. I was a husband to them but they broke that agreement.*'[4]

We flinch, recalling the Lover's heartbreak.

'*This is the agreement I will make with the people of Israel… I will forgive them for the wicked things they did, and I will not remember their sins anymore.*'[5]

A release of ecstasy rushes up through our body. This

is the pivotal moment again. Yahweh's everlasting era of goodness will be possible because all sins will be forgiven. Forgiveness will be covenanted, contracted, promised for all time.

But how?

What will happen to make this possible?

We lift up the Jeremiah page by its top hinge:

Holding up a cup of wine, Jesus declares, *'This is my blood,* the new covenant, *poured out for many for the forgiveness of sins.'*[6]

Stunned by the revelation, we stagger back to the centre of the room and, turning full circle, we gaze in amazement at the Rescue Mission so far.

Until now the blood of an animal has been offered in place of the punishment that humans deserve. This was forgiveness. This was Love and Justice holding hands.

But now... now there will be a new blood poured out for the forgiveness of sins.

It is promised.

It is covenanted.

There will be blood.

Jesus' blood.

And it is non-negotiable.

It is cold and late, starlight flickers off the greenery, and an arousing perfume of foliage surrounds. Peter nods in gentle appreciation: Gethsemane is the perfect

atmospheric setting for the drama about to unfold.
'Sit here while I pray.'[7]
Peter can hear the nerves in Jesus' voice; the apprehension, the vulnerability, the fear. He sees the beads of sweat sliding over the hills and valleys of Jesus' grimaced brow. This is it. Tonight, at long last, the battle for Jerusalem begins. Jesus needs you tonight, Peter tells himself. Keep your guard; do not fall asleep.

Jesus heads off into the trees and the moment he disappears from sight, all his composure crumbles. His legs give way and Jesus crashes to the ground, kicking up a tower of dust. Dragging his face through the dirt, scraping his fingers through the ground, Jesus lets out a thunderous terrifying howl, sending birds flapping in the treetops.

Jesus is foaming at the mouth. *'Abba, Father! You can do all things. Take away this cup of suffering.'*[8]

Ruach clings onto Abba, never letting go. Tears stream from their eyes.

There will be blood.
Jesus' blood.
And it is negotiated.

Jesus' sweat has turned blood red.[9] It looks like every blood vessel will burst through his skin.
Straining for every breath, Jesus gasps, *'yet not what I will, but what you will.'*[10]

Not what I want.

What you want.

Surrounded by a paradise of greenery, the first humans rejected Elohim's will. They tore a schism between humanity and their passionate Creator.

Surrounded by a paradise of greenery, Jesus surrenders.

For the restoration of paradise.

For the renewal of relationship.

There will be blood.

Jesus' blood.

And it is chosen.

Jesus repeats his cry with increasing vigour long into the night. Throughout it all, Ruach clings tightly to Jesus, never letting go. She kisses his forehead, his cheeks, his nose, his lips. 'Oh, Yeshua, I am with you, my dear. *In the last days,*[11] our children *will beat their swords into ploughshares and their spears into pruning hooks.*[12] Nations will not *train for war anymore.*[13] All swords will be put away.'

By the time Jesus returns to his followers, the dust of the ground is pummelled into his fists, ingrained in his elbows and knees, and flung across his face.

The ground rumbles.

Peter stirs from his slumber. His eyes open to an approaching orange glow, and in a flash he is on his feet, positioned offensively, sword piercing the air in front. Emerging through the trees, with torches blazing, is a band of armoured soldiers.

Next to the soldiers stand several Jewish priests.

And in front of them all: Judas.

'Arghhhhhhhh,' Peter lunges forward, swinging wildly.

Metal crashes into metal in a frenetic melee.

'Stop! No more of this.'[14]

Jesus' roar cuts through the night.

'Put your sword away![15] *All who use swords will be killed with swords.'*[16]

Peter looks into his master's eyes in utter bewilderment.

'Surely, Peter, you know I could ask my Father, and he would give me more than twelve armies of angels.'[17]

Peter's shoulders fall in surrender.

His weapon slowly slips from his hand.

1. Jeremiah 31:9
2. Jeremiah 31:20
3. Jeremiah 31:31 (NIV)
4. Jeremiah 31:32
5. Jeremiah 31:33–34
6. Matthew 26:28 (NIV)
7. Mark 14:34
8. Mark 14:36
9. Luke 22:44
10. Mark 14:36 (NIV)
11. Isaiah 2:2
12. Isaiah 2:4 (NIV)
13. Isaiah 2:4
14. Luke 22:51
15. John 18:11
16. Matthew 26:52
17. Matthew 26:52–53

5.10 – Kingdoms on Earth

Ratio, rhythm and routine are rooted in the very essence of the created order. But even for the sun, so accustomed to daily ritual, today will be no ordinary day.

Jerusalem wakes with excitement as the first morning rays, and the crow of a cockerel, announce the arrival of Passover. Children rush into the streets, dancing and singing, expressing a joy so universal even Roman soldiers cannot stifle a smile.

Standing in stark contrast, High Priest Caiaphas is a picture of frustration. His interrogation of Jesus has gone on through the night; and so far, all attempts to acquire convincing convicting evidence have merely resulted in a conflicting web of contradictions. Rising to his feet, Caiaphas bears down on his prisoner and with an aggravated snap he yells in Jesus' face, '*Are you the Christ, the Son of the blessed God*?'[1]

An arrow branches off from Caiaphas' question, directing us toward a Phase Four prophecy received during Babylonian exile.

'*In my vision*,' wrote Daniel, 'there *was one like a son of man, coming with the clouds of heaven. He approached the Ancient of Days and was led into his presence. He was given authority, glory and sovereign power; all peoples, nations and men of every language worshipped him. His dominion is*

*an everlasting dominion... his kingdom is one that will
never be destroyed.'*[2]
We read through the words carefully, not wanting to
miss anything. In this vision, a man enters the presence
of Yahweh and is given power over the earth. The man
is worshipped as if he is Yahweh himself.
Shocking.
Controversial.
Inflammatory.
Daniel's *face became white from fear.*[3]
Because he had seen the ultimate blasphemy.

'Are you going to answer? I'll ask you one final time.
Are you the Christ?'
Jesus leans closer into Caiaphas' face.
*'I am. And in the future you will see the Son of Man sitting
at the right hand of God, the Powerful One, and coming on
clouds in the sky.'*[4]
Fury explodes.
'Kill him!' Caiaphas screeches.
This is Daniel's vision.
This is the ultimate blasphemy.
Fists and saliva fly into Jesus.
And the day's first drop of blood drips to the floor.

'But, but...' we stutter desperately. 'This isn't
blasphemy. This is truth. Jesus was conceived by the
breath of Ruach. He is divine. He can enter God's
presence.'
Nobody seems able to hear us.

Lost in the silence, we feel totally confused. We feel convinced that Jesus is about to accomplish the Rescue Mission's most important victory. Yet we have no idea how. We understand that Jesus is the new covenant. We understand that Jesus will shed some of his blood for the forgiveness of sins, putting an end to the punishments that Justice demands, guaranteeing an unending era of kindness.

But forgiveness won't do it all; forgiveness won't ensure an everlasting paradise, will it? Ever since the first humans ate from the forbidden tree, their descendants have done the same, over and over and over again. Forgiveness won't stop humans from diminishing the beauty of the new kingdom, will it?

Jesus' kingdom must be free from all temptation.

Paradise must contain no knowledge of good and evil.

All evil must be purged; defeated and destroyed once and for all.

Another arrow branches off from Daniel's vision, leading us back to the narrative of Jesus' self-imposed exile in the desert.

'The devil took Jesus and showed him all the kingdoms of the world.'

We freeze. Devil? Who is this devil?

'The devil said to Jesus, "I will give you all these kingdoms and all their power and glory. It has been given to me, and I can give it to anyone I wish."'[5]

In Daniel's vision, the Son of Man will be given an unrelenting, indestructible kingdom. So who is this devil currently possessing kingdoms on Earth?

The arrows on the wall keep coming; they seem to be forming a trail.

'The kingdom of heaven is like a man who planted good seed in a field. That night, when everyone was asleep, his enemy came and planted weeds among the wheat.'[6] Jesus then explains, *'The field is the world... the good seeds are all of God's children... and the enemy who planted the bad seed is the devil.'*[7]

The devil is the enemy, the tempter in the garden, planter of bad seed; the one who lures humans away from choosing life. Creation has been hijacked; blindfolded; tied up and held to ransom.

This is the horrific, despicable work of the Hijacker.

The Hijacker has stolen power, stolen dominion over the earth. The Hijacker parades and marauds, wickedly licking his lips, revelling in his possession.

It is not the Romans that Jesus is confronting. The continuing trail of arrows reveal that Jesus is waging war against the Hijacker's kingdom, winning every battle so far. Demon by demon, Jesus is overthrowing the enemy's legions.[8] Demon by demon, Jesus is liberating and healing,[9] restoring the kingdom of God.[10] Demon by demon, the enemy is falling like lightning from the heavens.[11]

We feel faint, light-headed, overwhelmed by the sheer scale of Jesus' ambition. From a Roman revolution to the end of all evil, our understanding of Jesus' mission has just exploded exponentially. The Hijacker's kingdom must be destroyed for evermore.

Only then will paradise reign.

1. Mark 14:61
2. Daniel 7:13-14 (NIV)
3. Daniel 7:28
4. Mark 14:62
5. Luke 4:5-7
6. Matthew 13:24-25
7. Matthew 13:38-39
8. Mark 5:8-9
9. Luke 13:16
10. Luke 11:20
11. Luke 10:18

5.11 – For He Has Won

Our thoughts are a muddle, our emotions a mess. With blasphemy commonplace, accepted within Roman culture, High Priest Caiaphas is instead trying to convince the authorities that Jesus is a political threat, a potent revolutionary.

But this is the man who roared, 'Put away your sword'. Jesus cannot be found guilty.

Surely.

And yet we know how the Rescue Mission works by now: the more perilous the plight, the more dramatic the escape, the more memorable the rescue. Phase Three's Egyptian liberation wouldn't still be emblazoned on our mind if the waves hadn't parted at the last possible moment, when all hope was lost, when death was imminent.

We fear for Jesus. We fear a miscarriage of justice.

But we are in no doubt: Jesus will not be killed.

'You brought this man to me saying he makes trouble among the people,' Governor Pilate proclaims to the swarming masses below his balcony. *'But I have questioned him before you all, and I have not found him guilty.'*[1]

There is an audible intake of breath.

Before complete and utter bedlam.

Fists shake in derision, missiles soar through the air.

Pilate cannot understand it. He has just acquitted one

of the crowd's own, pardoned a Jewish challenger of Rome; they should be celebrating. Yet Pilate can see the hatred in Caiaphas' eyes; he is whipping up this storm. For some reason, and Pilate has no idea why, Caiaphas needs Jesus dead.

The irony is not lost on Pilate: declaring Jesus not guilty of starting an uprising, could have inadvertently started an uprising. In no time at all, this riot could disseminate into chaos and a bloody crackdown on the Jewish people. And at Passover as well; how would that look?

Pilate rolls his eyes.

He is cornered with no room for manoeuvre.

Jesus will have to be punished severely.

Whipped.

Flogged.

But he will not be killed.

Pilate could never allow such an injustice.

Throughout it all Jesus stands motionless, heart beating with passionate love. Residing in human flesh, Yahweh stares straight into the eyes of his people, seeing only contempt, disdain and derision all around. After millennia of conveying his affection, here Love stands receiving nothing but the vilest hatred. His back tenses and straightens preparing for the physical agony about to join the emotional suffering already underway.

There will be blood.

Jesus' blood.

And it is chosen.

As if positioned for prayer, Jesus kneels naked with hands tied to a post, his whole body shuddering in trepidation. When the first thwack of leather lashes bare back, shards of metal simultaneously cling like claws. Having taken hold they dig deep then tug.

And scrape.

And rip.

And tear.

Hurling chunks of flesh to the floor below.

Blood quickly follows, spraying out in a parabola.

And again.

And again.

Soon Jesus kneels in a pool of his own blood and flesh. Eyes shut tighter than they've ever been shut before.

Cling. Mother, brothers, sisters, this is for you.

Tug. For each precious friend: those watching on distraught; those who have fled in fear.

Tear. For you Abba, for you Ruach.

With teeth clenched so tight they grind, Jesus can hold it in no longer. The audible manifestation of agony shoots from the throat: short, sharp shrieks followed by exhausted heavy panting, as though of a dog; then one long howl.

Kneeling in a puddle of our tears, hands clenched tightly, we flinch as each blow of the whip grips, rips and shreds Jesus. 'MAKE IT STOP!' we roar. 'Stop. Now. Please. Do something!'

As if responding to our cry, a piece of paper floats down from the Phase Four rafters, rocking back and forth through the air. We intercept its fall and open up a note written by Isaiah: *'I offered my back to those who beat me.'*[2]

Our head shakes in bewilderment.

'But that's enough. There must be enough. Stop! Please. There must be enough blood already for the new covenant, for the forgiveness of sins.'

With every patch of skin on Jesus' back either ripped off or hidden under a layer of dripping blood, the whippings finally stop. A kick to the ribs further enrages the seething pain of Jesus' open wounds. Jesus feels on fire when, finally, to complete his humiliation, a crown of thorns is shoved on his head, causing parallel lines of blood to race down his face.

Now there's enough.

Now it has finished.

Surely.

Please, Abba, please.

Jesus' shattered limp body is dragged next to a bulky slobbering brute named Barabbas. Pilate will offer the crowds a choice. One of these men will be freed as a goodwill Passover offering.[3] It's the unpunished but guilty versus the mutilated but innocent.

Violence against non-violence.

Murder or surrender?

'I have Barabbas and Jesus. Which do you want me to set free for you?'

'Barabbas.'
'So what should I do with Jesus, the one you call Christ?'
'Crucify him!'
'Why? What wrong has he done?'
'Crucify him!'[4]

We cannot cope with the suspense any longer. Angered by the insanity of it all, feeling like we are going to be sick, we are just desperate to learn of Jesus' fate, desperate to discover how Jesus will be rescued.
Skipping large chunks of narrative, our eyes flick down the wall.

It was about noon and the whole land became dark until three o'clock in the afternoon because the sun did not shine. Then Jesus cried out in a loud voice, 'Father, I give you my life.'
After Jesus said this, he died.[5]

Shaking our head with mouth wide open we stumble back, only to lose our footing and crash to the floor. No, no, no, it cannot be. The room plunges into darkness. Our body runs cold; vomit falls from our mouth. Never before have we felt so distraught, so afraid, so vulnerable, so alone.
With God's ultimate plan slaughtered...
There will be... no... rescue.
The Mission has failed.
And the Hijacker skips and jumps with wicked glee, for he has won.

1. Luke 23:14
2. Isaiah 50:6
3. John 18:39

4. Matthew 27:21-23
5. Luke 23:44-46

5.12 – When Darkness Rules

Staring straight up into a black abyss, arms and legs spread out like a star, we lay motionless and numb, absent of all emotion.

As the minutes - perhaps hours - trudge slowly by, ever so gradually our senses return. It is freezing cold, we lie soaking in a puddle, and we can smell our own vomit.

Full of pain, we choose to return to our trance.

At least it is safe there.

At least it hurts less there.

'This is your time - the time when darkness rules.'[1]

A loud but fractured voice shakes us from our daze. Only now does an aching, distressed, almost childlike groan come, bringing with it the first wave of tears. Rolling up into a ball, clutching our neck, tense and taut, our mourning begins.

'It's all over' we bellow again and again, between heavy, rasping breaths. Grieving the end of hope, we thump the ground in anger, discovering that the freezing temperatures have turned our pool of tears to ice. Because dignity no longer matters, we take hold of our clothing and start to rip.

And tear.

And shred.

Clunk, clunk.

The sound is of something metallic falling to the ice.

Scrambling in the dark, we locate the small cylindrical torch which successfully - but now pointlessly - guided us through the Phase Four loft.

Switching the instrument on, our eyes battle to adjust. Although blurred by our tears, we are able to make out numerous scraps of paper scattered across the floor. Scrambling on all fours, we pick up each scrap. And for several minutes we just sit there, papers in hand, refusing to engage.

Why should we?

It's just not worth it any more.

It's all over.

But eventually.

Eventually, with a heavy heart, we lay out the pieces of paper and spot that they can be placed into two piles: those 'Written by David' - lyrics from a song, we assume - and those 'By Isaiah.'

We take a deep breath. Convinced that only further misery awaits, we summon the courage to engage with our grief. Shining the torch towards the Phase Five wall, we illuminate the text that we skipped: the final hours of Jesus' life.

Outside Jerusalem's city walls, at a place known as 'The Skull,' Jesus hangs on two wooden beams, his arms spread along the horizontal, legs dropping down the vertical. Nails fix him in place, hammered through his hands and feet.

Only able to use his arms to lift his body, every breath is utterly exhausting.

Fatigue will be the most likely cause of death.
If blood loss or dehydration don't strike first.

Shining the torch down to the paper in our hand, we read, *'My heart is like wax; it has melted inside me. My strength has dried up like a clay pot, and my tongue sticks to the top of my mouth.'*[2]

'I am thirsty,'[3] Jesus gasps as another wave of weeping and wailing washes over his friends and family.
But for others watching on, Jesus' suffering brings much hilarity. Revelling in their power, relishing crushing the one who claimed such greatness, they mock and taunt, urging Jesus to save himself.
Yet still Jesus hangs.

David wrote, *'I am like a worm instead of a man. People make fun of me and hate me... They say, "Turn to* Yahweh *for help. Maybe he will save you."'*[4]
We double-take, as the seed of a formidable possibility drops into our heart.

Delirious soldiers sit competing for a memento from their day's achievements, throwing lots to win Jesus' bloodied clothes.[5]

The next paper in our hand reads, *'They divided my clothes among them, and they threw lots for my clothing.'*[6]
Our head shakes in shock.
Surely not.

It cannot be.

We check the next piece.

'They have pierced my hands and feet.'[7]

No way. This is too much to take.

Did David really write about this day, centuries before crucifixion was even conceived?

With physical, emotional and spiritual persecution firing through every sinew of his being, Jesus turns to King David's most angst-ridden lyrics, to fully express - fully encapsulate - his most excruciating wound.

Summoning every last breath, Jesus cries to the heavens, *'My God, my God, why have you rejected me?'*[8]

The most excruciating wound is rejection.

Disconnection crushes the heart.

Jesus feels abandoned.

Abandoned by Abba.

Abandoned by Ruach.

Separated from the one who breathes life, Jesus roars in agony.

Then breathes out for the final time.

Our body shakes in an eruption of pent-up pain. Absorbed by the Rescuer's constant longing for relationship we connect with the ultimate disconnection.

We mourn separation.

We weep for Jesus' loss.

A Roman soldier approaches Jesus' limp body and, like

a butcher in a slaughterhouse, stabs his spear into the flesh.[9]

'They will look on me, the one they have stabbed...'

The stilted, struggling, strained voice fills the Headquarters. The voice is strikingly real. It is not in our head. It is with us, around us, surrounding us, moving us to tears.

'...and they will cry like someone crying over the death of an only child. They will be as sad as someone who has lost a firstborn son.'[10]

We weep for Abba's loss.

1. Luke 22:53
2. Psalm 22:14-15
3. John 19:28
4. Psalm 22:8
5. John 19:23-24
6. Psalm 22:18
7. Psalm 22:16 (NIV)
8. Psalm 22:1
9. John 19:34
10. Zechariah 12:10

5.13 – There Can Be No Relationship

But for the Phase Four prophecies in our hands we could have wept for hours. Absorbing our tears, soon to become illegible, a second pile of papers demand our urgent attention.

'He was beaten down and punished,' the first piece reads, *'but he didn't say a word. He was like a lamb being led to be killed.'*[1]

Our head bows. This prophecy by Isaiah, written seven centuries before Jesus' death, sufficiently describes his surrender. An annotation explains that the lamb prepared for the annual Passover feast was always without fault: unmarked, with no broken bones.

We look up again at the crucifixion narrative on the wall and read of the fate of two convicted criminals on either side of Jesus' spiritless frame. To speed up the men's deaths, soldiers pummel their legs with metal, smashing and cracking until their bones shatter.[2]

No longer able to lift themselves to breathe, they shall be dead in moments.

Turning to face Jesus, the soldiers drop their weapons. They do not need to *break his legs... he* is *already dead.*[3]

Threads pull together in our mind.

No broken bones, killed at Passover, slaughtered like a lamb: was… was… was Jesus' death deliberately like that of a Passover lamb?

'He was buried with wicked men... He had done nothing

wrong, and he had never lied.'[4]

We nod in recognition. Jesus was unmarked, unblemished, completely without fault.

The ultimate, definitive Passover lamb.

During Moses' Egyptian liberation, the smeared blood of a lamb protected the Israelites from judgment and death. Was the original Passover a model, a sign, a forerunner of something far greater? Has Jesus' death always been part of the plan?

Was the Messiah's mission to die?

Was Jesus destined for death?

'It was Yahweh *who decided to crush him and make him suffer.'*[5]

'But... but... but...' we stutter. The thought is just too much to take in. The question, finally forced out through blubbering splutters, is too much to contemplate: 'But why?'

As if dreading its contents, we peer down at the next Isaiah quotation.

'He took our suffering on him and felt our pain for us.'[6]

For us.

Jesus took the punishment - for us.

He took the death that we deserve.

That we deserve.

Like a volcanic eruption, memories explode up from our depths.

Words which suffocated life.

Thoughts which smothered beauty.

Actions which smacked against justice.

And most of all, for we have even done it in this room,

we are struck by our constant ignoring and denial of God's presence, our rejection of Love, our rejection of relationship.

It is sin which holds Jesus to the wooden beams.

The world's sin.

And our sin.

We killed Jesus.

Falling onto all fours again, we stare down at the iced floor. Torchlight shines on the surface, causing the ice to act as a mirror. Dilated and bloodshot, our eyes are smeared with guilt.

Then we notice the blood.

The palms of our hands are dripping.

'Father.'

A flash of fear shoots through our aching body.

'Father.'

The voice is the one that we heard earlier, the one in the room with us, permeating through us. Fearing judgement and condemnation, fearing retribution and punishment, we peer nervously upward.

'Father, forgive them, because they do not know what they are doing.'[7]

Our head drops down to the ice. Only one word is on our mind. It rumbles around inside of us, increasing in energy before spewing out: 'Sorry.'

Again and again we spit out the word, each repetition flowing with increasing ease.

What happens next is a sight we shall never forget. Colour returning to our cheeks, dark stains lifting from around our eyes, we slowly lift up our hands and stare straight into our palms.

The blood has gone.

Eyes open wide, face fresh with amazement, we want to thank the voice; we want to see the voice. But silence has returned. We are alone again.

'He willingly gave his life,' Isaiah writes, *'and was treated like a criminal. But he carried away the sins of many people and asked forgiveness for those who sinned.'*[8]

A seed of hope is germinating within us: perhaps Jesus' death isn't the end after all?

We rise to our feet and look again at the crucifixion narrative. We read about an enormous embroidered curtain which, for almost a thousand years, served as a blockade in Jerusalem's Temple, protecting dirt-stained humans from perishing in God's spotless holiness.

No-one was allowed beyond the curtain into the Most Holy Place.

With the exception of one man, once a year.

When entering with blood as an offering for sin.

To our amazement, we discover that the curtain now lies crumpled in a heap. Ripped from top to bottom - a physically impossible feat - the curtain crashed to the ground at precisely the moment that Jesus let out his final breath.[9] We are told, 'Jesus *entered the Most Holy Place only once - and for all time. He did not take with him the blood of goats and calves. His sacrifice was his own blood and by it he set us free from sin forever.'*[10]

We want to put our hands in the air to dance and celebrate. At long last, relationship is possible. Now humans can enter God's spotless, beautiful presence

because they are spotless and beautiful too. This is the breakthrough that Elohim has craved for millennia.
But we cannot dance.
We cannot celebrate.
Not when darkness still surrounds.
When darkness rules, there can be no relationship.
Because Elohim remains dead in the grave.

1. Isaiah 53:7
2. John 19:32
3. John 19:33
4. Isaiah 53:9
5. Isaiah 53:10
6. Isaiah 53:4
7. Luke 23:34 (NIV)
8. Isaiah 53:12
9. Matthew 27:51
10. Hebrews 9:12

5.14 – Both Hug Tight

With the lip quivering, like it will give way at any moment, Thomas sits crumpled in a corner, cutting a bitter and twisted figure. This devastated disciple of Jesus is beyond tears; they've all been buried deep inside beneath a pile of resentment and regret.

Thomas has been counting the days since hope was executed. Today is Monday. Ten agony filled days have passed since everything truly worth living for was snatched from before his eyes. He'd truly believed that Jesus could overthrow the Romans. The miracles - and even the words - had been so convincing.

Maybe Jesus believed it too? He always seemed so sincere. Maybe Jesus fell for his own hype as well?

Instead of resenting Jesus, Thomas blames himself. This entire nightmare could have been spared if he'd just stopped Jesus getting too ambitious.

Alongside the head-spinning muddle of analysis, Thomas is also mourning the tragic loss of a great friend. Nobody so young, nobody so innocent, deserves to die like that.

But it's all over now.

It has finished.

This was no Messiah.

In the same room, the other ten members of Jesus' inner circle sit together separate from Thomas. In the last week, Thomas has seen each one completely lose the plot. The grief has sent them insane. A week ago they all claim to have seen Jesus alive.

Like, actually alive!

It's only natural, Thomas muses, to see what you want to see when mourning.

Peter and John defend their insanity, arguing that Jesus' tomb is empty.[1] But that means nothing; the body could have been stolen.[2]

And Mary Magdalene even claims to have had a one-to-one conversation with him.[3] But she's always been a touch crazy.[4]

Again and again, with incessant excitement and animation, they all told Thomas, *'We saw the Lord.'*[5]

Refusing to believe may leave him increasingly isolated and ignored, but Thomas is going nowhere. As the only one left of sound mind he must keep them safe, and ensure everyone keeps a low profile until their crazed spell wears off. All failed revolutionaries could well be the next targets on the Roman hit list.

Thomas double checks again: the doors are locked.

They are safe.

'I will not believe it until I see the nail marks in his hands and put my finger where the nails were.'[6] The sentence has run through Thomas' mind on loop, ever since he first angrily snapped each word with great assertiveness.

Tightly clutching bent knees close to his chest, he whispers the words again, 'I will not believe. Until...'

All of a sudden Thomas sees everyone jump to their feet as the volume rapidly rises.

'What is it now?' he shrugs with frustration, struggling to fathom out the fuss.

And then he sees it.

He sees him.

Jesus stands in the room.

In sheer disbelief, Thomas looks to the locked doors:[7] how? This isn't possible. No-one can enter the room.

Despite rising to his feet for further inspection, Thomas has already made up his mind over the mystery. This figure looking like Jesus must be a ghost or some sort of mirage, which means he too has finally been infected with insanity.

Thomas moves closer. All peripheral vision fades into irrelevance as he finds himself increasingly mesmerized by a figure of overwhelming beauty, and definite likeness to Jesus.

But Jesus had never been one blessed with good looks.[8]

This could be a ghost.

I will not believe.

Until I see.

Until I touch.

Love radiates from Jesus' radiant eyes, and Thomas feels every knot inside begin to loosen. A warm glowing sensation takes over the pit of his stomach, which spreads rapidly through his whole body when Jesus opens his mouth and familiar, much missed tones are heard.

'Put your finger here, and look at my hands.'[9]

A champion's smile beams at Thomas, as Jesus holds out his hands.

Revealing nail scarred wrists.

Fingers gently caress Jesus' forearm, slowly stroking down towards his hand; but before reaching the palm they slide effortlessly into, and find rest within, the hole. Thomas looks up, his face a picture of amazement, wonder and awe.

And Jesus continues to smile knowingly.

Taking hold of both wrists, placing a thumb in each crevice, Thomas smiles back. His inner mountain of resentment and regret crumbles away, setting free tears of joy trickling down.

After a couple of minutes, a fully settled and certain Thomas loosens his grip from the wrists, allowing Jesus to reach upward and tenderly wipe the tears from his friend's cheek before embracing.

Both hug tight.

This can be no ghost.

Thomas can have no doubt.

Because it is true: Jesus is alive.

After the most brutal, torturous death, Jesus is alive.

Where death had triumphed, life now bursts forth to deliver the knockout blow. Evil kicks and screams in writhing agony. Because, with the Hijacker's ultimate achievement comprehensively conquered, there will be rescue.

The Mission has succeeded.

And Yahweh jumps and dances and embraces with sheer delight and ecstasy, for he has won.

1. John 20:3-7
2. Matthew 28:12-13
3. John 20:18
4. Luke 8:2
5. John 20:25
6. John 20:25
7. John 20:26
8. Isaiah 53:2
9. John 20:27

5.15 – A Question

Into the darkness of night, a light rises. The golden sunbeams of daybreak reflect off Lake Galilee's surface, causing it to shimmer and shine. On the water, a small fishing vessel floats calmly; on board, two friends stand staring at the horizon, basking in the rays of the rising sun.

'That's how I felt when I saw him,' Thomas grins at Peter. 'His light overcame my darkness.'[1]

Hands fall forcefully on the pair's shoulders.

'It is the Lord! *It is the Lord!*'[2]

Like an excited child, John is pointing across the water.

Sure enough, Peter and Thomas can see the figure standing on the shore and without a moment's hesitation, Peter is in the lake, swimming frenetically to the shore.

Jesus ushers Peter in with open arms.

'Are you hungry, my friend?'

The mundane question catches Peter by surprise. He looks down to see fish frying on *a fire of hot coals*.[3]

'Take a seat. Here, try this one.'

Peter has to pinch himself as time slips by.

The conversation.

The friendship.

So easy, so familiar, so ordinary.

As if nothing had happened.

With their breakfast on the beach consumed to full satisfaction, the Rescuer can hold it in no more; Jesus is simply desperate to ask Peter a question, one burning deep within. It's a question that Yahweh has been asking for millennia. It's a question that has been beating with fervent passion at the very core of Love. And now, thanks to Jesus' ultimate triumph, the entire Rescue Mission has been stripped to its heartbeat.

Jesus asks, *'Do you love me?'*[4]

At the very moment that we read of Thomas touching the holes in Jesus' wrists, glorious light filled the Headquarters, illuminating every corner of the room. We peer down at the final Phase Four prophecy in our hand: *'After his soul suffers many things,'* Isaiah declared, *'he will see life and be satisfied.'*[5]

Stretching our arms out in triumph we spin round on the spot. These feel like the first moments of love: the instant attraction, the free-flowing conversation, the look in the eyes, the hours feeling like minutes; if only it could last like this forever.

The ice beneath our feet is melting; the water evaporating. Decades of dust and dirt are lifted into the air, revealing further narratives splayed out across the Headquarters floor. And painted bright in the centre of it all, imprinted at the heart of Phase Six, Jesus promises, *'Because I live, you will live too.'*[6]

1. Ephesians 5:8
2. John 21:7
3. John 21:9
4. John 21:16
5. Isaiah 53:11
6. John 14:19

PHASE SIX

6.01 – Let There Be Light

In the beginning was the Word.
The Word was with God and the Word was God.[1]
The earth was formless and empty.[2]
Then the Word spoke into the darkness, *'Let there be light.'*
And there was light.[3]
The Word was in the world.
And the world was made by him.
But the world did not know him.
So *the Word* took on flesh.[4]

And wherever the Word breathed, beauty arose.

Every word brought revelation and healing, equality and forgiveness. Eyes opened to the possibility of a whole new way of living. Minds awakened to the prospect of a better world.

Ever since Ruach first breathed life into humans, Love has sought collaboration and relationship. *'Be fruitful and increase in number,'* was Elohim's passionate plea. *'Fill the earth and subdue it. Rule over the fish in the sea and the birds in the air and over every living creature.'*[5]

Crafted in the image of their Creator, humans were invited to share creative responsibility. They were commissioned to cultivate, nurture and conserve.

Every act of construction.

Distribution.

Education.

Development.

Management.

Organisation.

Administration.

It all serves to bring order to chaos.

And now the time has come for the resurrected Jesus to add to the original creation mandate. Standing with his followers on the mountaintops, the air bracing, the view expansive, Jesus stretches his arms to the skies and declares, *'You will be my witnesses in Jerusalem, in all Judea and Samaria, and to the ends of the earth.*[6] *All authority in heaven and earth has been given to me. Therefore go and make disciples of all nations.'*[7]

At the dawn of a new creation - after Mary mistook Jesus for a gardener[8] - *the firstborn from among the dead*[9] invites his followers to share creative responsibility. Equipped with every power in the universe, Love seeks collaboration.

'I am the light of the world,'[10] Jesus proclaims, before leaning forward into the ear of his Bride and whispering, *'You are the light of the world.*[11] Now let there be light!'

Clouds gather around Jesus as he rises into the air.[12]

And then he is gone, visible no more.

At first, Peter grieves for his master, his friend, his life's purpose, all over again. But as the days pass, Jesus' parting words begin to soothe and massage, then invigorate and energise.

Now Peter stands as the epitome of expectation. Ten days on from Jesus' ascension, Peter sways from side to side, bold and brash, imploring his friends to stay strong. 'We saw Daniel's vision - Jesus, the Son of Man travelling up into the clouds - we saw it plain before our eyes. That's how we can be sure that he is reigning with all *"authority, glory and power"*.'[13]

Peter's arms swing with excitement.

'The wait is nearly over. Jesus promised to provide a *Counsellor to be with* us *forever.*[14] *When the Holy Spirit comes*, we *will receive power.*'[15]

No one in the room dares disagree. Their lives are on hold.

Waiting.

Waiting.

Not even the raucous celebrations of Pentecost, blaring from the streets below, will disturb their focus.

Waiting.

Waiting.

Waiting.

Suddenly a sound like a violent wind[16] crashes through the house. Ruach rushes and swirls, shaking those in her midst, igniting ferocious flames of fire. Then, like she did in the very first humans, like she did in Moses' tabernacle and Solomon's Temple, Ruach enters, settles down and makes herself at home. Jesus' followers become *the temple of the living God.*[17]

Jesus died and rose again at Passover - the annual celebration of Moses' Egyptian liberation. And fifty days later, Ruach has descended at Pentecost - the annual celebration of Moses receiving Yahweh's laws; laws designed to help a new, emerging, liberated society to flourish.

Every year at Pentecost the first fruit of the year's harvest would be offered to Yahweh. This year it is Yahweh who makes the offering.

Love.

Joy.

Peace.

Patience.

Kindness.

Goodness.

Faithfulness.

Gentleness.

Self-control.[18]

The fruit of Ruach will help a new, emerging, liberated society to flourish. Working in intimate relationship, her character inside lives will transform lives.

Abba holds Yeshua under his right arm and kisses his Son in pure tender affection. A stunning serenade surrounds, singing over and over, *'The Lamb who was killed is worthy to receive power, wealth, wisdom and strength, honour, glory and praise!'*[19]

Delight soars within Father and Son as they watch Peter - totally transformed from the fisherman they once knew - bellow to the bustling Pentecost crowds, *'God raised Jesus from the dead.*[20] *Change your hearts and lives and be baptised, each one of you… receive the Holy*

Spirit.'[21]

Yeshua shines with sheer elation as Jews from Egypt, Arabia, Mesopotamia, Asia, Crete, even Rome, all respond to Peter's call; all in Jerusalem for the Pentecost festivities.

Abba's heart summersaults in excitement as this new society, overflowing with the fruit of Ruach, starts to reflect his own character. Justice and equality, compassion and generosity all come to the fore, with possessions shared by rich and poor alike.[22]

At the entrance to Jerusalem's Temple, Peter stops beside a man famous for having never walked a step in his life.

'By the power of Jesus,' Peter says with confidence, *'stand up and walk!'*[23]

New life is breathed into the man's ankles as he jumps to his feet.[24]

And takes his first steps on the earth.

This is restoration.

This is new life sprouting up.

This is the new creation blossoming.

This is the Word speaking into the darkness, 'Let there be light!'

And there is light.

1. John 1:1
2. Genesis 1:2
3. Genesis 1:3
4. John 1:14
5. Genesis 1:28
6. Acts 1:9
7. Matthew 28:18-19
8. John 20:15
9. Colossians 1:18
10. John 8:12
11. Matthew 5:14 (NIV)
12. Acts 1:9
13. Daniel 7:14
14. John 14:16 (NIV)
15. Acts 1:8
16. Acts 2:2
17. 2 Corinthians 6:16
18. Galatians 5:22-23
19. Revelation 5:12
20. Acts 2:2
21. Acts 2:38
22. Acts 2:45
23. Acts 3:6
24. Acts 3:8

6.02 – Crown of Flowers

With a ragged damp cloth, John gently dabs the congealing wounds strewn across Peter's back; a mottled patchwork of red, blue and black. It is like dousing a bed of sizzling coals. The water cools and stings in equal measure.

'The beatings are getting worse, Peter. Next time...'

A knock at the door cuts John short.

'Ignore it,' John urges.

But Peter is already on his feet, striding as best as he can across the room.

'Who is it?' Peter whispers through the doorframe.

'It's me, Philip. I got here as soon as I could. They didn't see me.'

Peter's relief dissolves the second he opens the door. John sees it too and immediately stands to his feet. Grief is etched across Philip's face.

'It's chaos out there,' Philip chokes. 'They're seizing us all over Jerusalem... and Stephen... Stephen...'

Peter and John look away, fearing the worst.

'Stephen... they killed him.'

'No!'

'They ran at him screaming, they grabbed him like... like... like a slab of meat. They dragged him out of Jerusalem and stoned him.'

'No!' Peter buckles forward, winded.

'But... but... why? What had he done?'

'It was blasphemy. Stephen said the same thing that Jesus said at his trial.'

'*In the future,*' says John, recalling Jesus' inflammatory words, '*you will see the Son of Man sitting at the right hand of God.*'[1]

'Yes, Stephen said that he could see it. He saw "*heaven open and the Son of Man standing at God's right side.*"[2] His face was shining in the presence of God. But the priests didn't seem to notice. Or care.'

The three bow their heads.

Together they stand in silence.

Simply paying their respects.

'Why?' Philip asks, brushing away his tears. 'Why are we suffering like this? If Jesus is reigning in glory, possessing every power in the universe, why doesn't he save us?'

Peter and John take their time before responding, choosing their words carefully. 'These are the first days of a whole new world,' Peter begins. 'But these are also *the last days*[3] of the old world.'

'It's as if the old is giving birth to the new,' adds John. 'God's Kingdom has begun. We've seen it. It's here, it's arrived. But it's like Jesus said: it's a seed that grows and grows and grows.'

'*We are waiting for a new heaven and a new earth where goodness lives.*[4] Only then will the Kingdom of God be seen in all its fullness.'

'Until then we have been *given the honour of suffering disgrace for Jesus.*[5] We must share *in Christ's sufferings;*[6] follow Jesus' example.'[7]

Philip nods, reminded of Stephen's final words; when Stephen cried out, *'Lord, do not hold this sin against them,'*[8] he was echoing Jesus' own dying plea.'[9]

'But... but...' says Philip, 'what if we all end up dead? What if they kill us all? What good would we be to Jesus then?'

Eyes heavy and piercing, determination and resolve envelope Peter.

'Jesus told us to go to Judea and Samaria, and to the ends of the earth, and we have to trust that he will get us there. God's plans never die. When our ancestors were exiled in Babylon, Jerusalem was in ruins, all hope seemed lost. Yet the King of Babylon was so impressed by our ancestors, he wrote to every nation in his kingdom and decreed, "Israel's God *is the living God; he lives forever. His kingdom will never...*"'[10]

Crash.

Thrown from its hinges, the front door is sent skidding across the floor. Standing in the doorway is Saul, their most relentless pursuer. Saul marches towards them, slashes Peter and John across the face then seizes Philip, pushing a blade up against his throat.

Philip looks Saul in the eye.

And prays blessing on his captor.

Bound in chains, Philip is hurled into the back of a wagon, tossed alongside hundreds captured for allegiance to Jesus.[11] Saul drives his prisoners to a hurting, barren land, where they can bother Jerusalem no more.

He leaves his exiles in Samaria, the humiliated former

capital of Israel.

'How terrible it will be for Samaria, the pride of Israel's drunken people!' Isaiah once prophesied. *'That beautiful crown of flowers is just a dying plant.'*[12]

And sure enough, like Jerusalem, Samaria experienced unmitigated annihilation. But unlike Jerusalem, Samaria never recovered from its destruction. Unlike Jerusalem, Samaria's exiles never returned home. Samaria appeared to have been rejected and abandoned, forever.

Forced out from Jerusalem to Samaria, dumped in the discarded city, Philip begins to proclaim *the Good News*[13] of Jesus. Hundreds respond to his message as Ruach swoops and swirls in delight, liberating and healing, breathing new life into her returning children. Restoring the dying plant of Israel into a beautiful crown of flowers.

1. Matthew 26:64
2. Acts 7:56
3. Acts 1:14
4. 2 Peter 3:13
5. Acts 5:41
6. 1 Peter 4:13
7. 1 Peter 2:21
8. Acts 7:60
9. Luke 23:34
10. Daniel 6:26
11. Acts 8:3-4
12. Isaiah 28:1
13. Acts 8:12

6.03 – The Academics of Athens

With the tip of his knife, Saul carefully slices through the fabric in his hand. He sits under the cover of his market-stall, engrossed in his work, almost oblivious to the bustling world around him. Tent making is simply a means to an end for Saul. For thirteen years, he has kept his head down, building his business, earning and saving money, and biding his time.

Rehearsing his proclamations.

Refining his arguments.

Processing his logic.

Preparing his evidence.

Shaping offences.

Structuring defences.

'How much for this one?'

Saul hardly looks up, simply glimpsing the object of enquiry.

'It's fifty for that one.'

'I'll give you a hundred.'

His attention caught, he puts his knife down and slowly looks up. A grin stretches across Saul's cheeks as he jumps to his feet, arms open for embrace. 'Barnabas, old friend, how are you? I've not seen you in years.'

'We're doing well thanks, Saul. You'll be pleased to hear Jesus' Kingdom is really spreading.'

'Oh, Barnabas, that is such good news.'

'But we think it's time to go further, Saul - much further. That's why I'm here. We need you. You're a Roman citizen, you speak Greek, you understand Greek culture, and you know the Jewish scriptures inside out. Oh, and you're from Tarsus - you'll know how to sail.'

'Barnabas,' says Saul, without a moment's hesitation. 'It would be an honour to travel with you. You were the first to forgive me for pursuing and persecuting you all. It would be a privilege to follow wherever you lead... Just how far were you thinking of going?'

Barnabas flashes his friend a playful smile.

'Let's just say you'd better start using your Roman name.'

'Right you are. In that case, I am Paul, at your service.'

Zeus.

Apollo.

Athena.

Neptune.

Ares.

Athena.

Feeling like Jonah must have done walking through Nineveh,[1] Paul roams the streets of Athens, feeling sick to the stomach, Ruach squirming inside him.[2] He has never seen so many monuments dedicated to gods. The city is saturated. It's no exaggeration: there are literally thousands of the things.

A theatre for Dionysus.

A stadium for Poseidon.

Athena.

Athena.

A temple for Neptune.

An altar *'TO A GOD WHO IS NOT KNOWN.'*[3]

Athena.

Athena.

Tears well in Paul's eyes as words of Isaiah clatter back and forth through his mind:

'A man cuts down a tree,

Burns half of the wood in the fire...

Then *makes a statue from the wood* leftover

And calls it his god.

He bows down to it and worships it.

He prays to it and says,

   "You are my God. Save me!"

It's as if their eyes are covered so they can't see.

Their minds don't understand...

They have not thought to themselves...

   "I am worshipping a block of wood!"'[4]

Before the days of Isaiah, the prophet Elijah challenged Canaan's god to set fire to a large pile of wood. The Canaanites cut their skin, desperately seeking Baal's attention. But after several hours they had failed to summon a single flame.

Elijah then drenched the wood with water, prayed out to Yahweh, and a raging fire blazed. *'If Baal really is a god, maybe he is thinking, or busy, or travelling! Maybe he is sleeping,'*[5] Elijah taunted.

Baal had no power.

Because Baal was just a chiselled block of wood.

Just like Zeus, Apollo and Athena.

There really is only one true God; one great universal God, who desires the hearts of every nation.

When Jonah visited Nineveh, God cared for the Ninevans; God forgave the Ninevans.[6]

Because *to God every person is the same.*[7]

There is no difference between Greeks and Jews.[8]

The only trouble is: the Greeks are not waiting for a Christ to liberate them.

They do not know the prophecies of Isaiah.

They were never ruled by David.

Never liberated by Moses.

Not fathered by Abraham.

How, Paul wonders, can he present Jesus as the climax of a millennia old story, when his audience does not know the story so far?

Worse still, at the heart of Paul's message is Jesus' physical, flesh and blood resurrection, returning to life in this world. The Greeks, by contrast, believe that only the human soul - not the body - lives on after death, in a solely spiritual realm.

And then there's the crucifixion - a stumbling block to Jews and Greeks alike.[9] The Greek mind can accept the notion of a god in human flesh - that's not an alien concept to them - but when Paul reveals that this divine flesh was slaughtered by human hands... well, they will just laugh.[10]

Because the gods do not suffer.

No god could ever be humiliated like that.

What could Paul possibly say that would change such

deeply ingrained convictions?

After all, Paul himself was not persuaded by arguments or personal testimony. It was only the direct intervention of Jesus, engulfing him in an explosion of pure blinding light, shouting, *'Saul, Saul! Why are you persecuting me?'*[11]

Paul has seen Jesus heal a crippled man in Lystra.[12]

He has seen Jesus shake the ground in Philippi.[13]

And in all cases, it was experiences coupled with explanation which revolutionised hearts and minds.

But what if there are no remarkable miracles today?

What if Paul is left with only words to convince the Greek intellectuals? What could he say?

Entering Athens' bustling marketplace, Paul gets to work, striking up several conversations.[14] And in a metropolis of ideas, open to change and advancement,[15] a crowd soon gathers around him. Before long, Paul is standing before Athens' most high-profile philosophers, the successors of Plato, Sophocles and Socrates.

'People of Athens,' Paul begins, Ruach breathing confidence within him, *'I can see you are very religious.* So I want to tell you about the God you do not know - *the God who made the whole world... the One who gives life, breath and everything else.'*[16]

As he speaks, Paul watches his audience intently.

In Thessalonica, he was hounded out of town.[17]

In Philippi, he was beaten and imprisoned.[18]

What will be the response from the academics of Athens?

1. Jonah 3:4
2. Acts 17:16
3. Acts 17:23
4. Isaiah 44:16-19
5. 1 Kings 18:27
6. Jonah 3:10
7. Acts 10:34
8. Colossians 3:11
9. 1 Corinthians 1:22-23
10. Acts 17:32
11. Acts 9:4
12. Acts 14:10
13. Acts 16:26
14. Acts 17:17
15. Acts 17:21
16. Acts 17:22-25
17. Acts 17:1-5
18. Acts 16:23

6.04 – Revolution is Complete

After three days of non-stop darkness, everything is moving but nothing is rhythmic. It's as if the ship is being thrown around by a sick and twisted nemesis: teasing and tormenting, tossing and turning in jagged pincer movements.

The winds are mighty and merciless.

The waves ride high and crash vehemently.

The rain swirls and lashes, drenching all in its wake.

And men sprint aimlessly, shrieking and flailing in futile panic.

Soldier, sailor, prisoner: all have given up hope.[1] Their battered brittle ship is being held together by rope.[2] It could shatter at any moment, sentencing all to the ravenous depths.

Resting in the arms of his Ruach, an elderly man sits quietly among the cargo.

I will make it to Rome, he prays.

I will make it to Rome.

You have promised it.[3]

I will meet with Caesar.

I will meet with Caesar.

Ruach gently massages the bald and bearded prisoner, comforting and reassuring, bringing peace to his bones. *'To live is Christ and to die is gain,'*[4] she whispers in the wind.

Though chained by his hands, the prisoner pushes down on a barrel and manages to force himself up to his feet. Fighting against the wind and rain, he stumbles forward.

'Stop! Stop!' he roars.

Heads turn on frantic, frenetic bodies, and on realising who it is shouting, pandemonium grinds to a halt. All have deep respect for this dishevelled impoverished prisoner. Despite decades of hardship, his warmth and generosity remain undiminished. They may not always agree with what he says, but whenever Paul speaks, everyone listens.

'Men, listen to me. *Last night an angel came to me* and *said, "Paul, do not be afraid. You must stand trial before Caesar."*[5] So *keep up your courage!*[6] *Not one of you will die; only the ship will be lost.*'[7]

Ruach dances around Yeshua and Abba, spinning with pure adoration. The trio of perfect love looks on in enthusiastic anticipation. After persuading the Roman authorities to have the case against Paul's imprisonment examined by Caesar himself,[8] after prompting them to pack Paul onto the next ship to Rome, they have been eagerly awaiting Paul's arrival.

With land in sight, Paul's fragile frame hits the seething seas. He is flung up and down, this way and that, before being dumped on the shore. Bodies and debris lay scattered across the sands.

Eight centuries ago, Isaiah provocatively prophesied: 'Yahweh *will show himself to the Egyptians, and then they will know he is* Yahweh. *They will worship God.*'[9] Isaiah's contemporaries were disgusted by the thought of the former enemy, former ruler, former oppressor falling in love with their Yahweh.

But here today, Elohim's heart is exploding with joy as Paul is welcomed into Rome by a thriving community of Romans; a community of Romans committed and devoted to Jesus; a community whose *faith is being reported all over the world.*[10]

Because the enemy.

The ruler.

The oppressor.

Is falling in love with Yahweh.

Thirty years ago in Jerusalem, the liberating Christ was expected to massacre the Roman enemy. He would be the greatest warrior of all time, the ultimate gladiator, an absolute master with the sword.

Yet Jesus roared, 'Put away your sword!'

His words stunned everyone.

And his non-violent approach to revolution was quickly crushed, quashed with sheer ease. He was slaughtered in the name of entertainment, suffering the most gruesome Roman execution.

Today, there are Romans in Rome proclaiming that 'Jesus is Lord.'[11] Each risks retribution for defying and denying Caesar's rule.

Walking through the city centre, Paul passes a temple for the Roman god Mars, another for the god Neptune, another for Saturn. And at the top of the hill he sees the largest of them all: the temple for Jupiter, king of the Roman pantheon. Sensing Elohim's aching heart in his creaking bones, it all reminds Paul of the scene of his greatest disappointment: his failure to convince the academics in Athens nearly two decades ago.

That really was a missed opportunity. With the support of the famous Greek philosophers, who knows how quickly the Good News of Jesus could have spread?

Sailing out from the selfish, promiscuous city of Corinth - carrying with him a contrasting message of faithful, sacrificial love - Paul has focussed his efforts on key influential cities.

Corinth was a centre of trade for the entire Roman Empire.

Thessalonica was the capital of Macedonia.

Athens was the former capital of the world.

And Rome is the new capital, the hub, the heart, the centre of it all.

Paul narrows his eyes, Ruach strengthening his resolve.

Soon he will meet with Caesar.

And this time, the opportunity shall not pass him by.

If he can just convince Caesar that Jesus is the one true Lord, reigning in glory over all the earth... well, the possibilities are endless. All roads lead to Rome; the ends of the earth could be reached in no time at all.

A sharp shooting pain pierces the pit of Paul's stomach when he hears an insatiable roar arising from inside an enormous, imperious stadium. Within the arena, two muscular men fight each other with flesh exposed, swords and shields clattering, in a no-holds-barred battle to the death. Thunder cracks across the skies as the deafening din of delirious crowds reaches a crescendo of celebration and the defeated gladiator is decapitated in the name of entertainment.

Rain lashes down as Ruach cries out in agony.

Grieving the loss of one she loves so dearly.

Sickened by the violence, so accepted and prevalent.

Longing for a better world of dignity and equality.

Paul falls to his knees and weeps with Ruach; there is still a long way to go before Jesus' non-violent revolution is complete.

1. Acts 27:20
2. Acts 27:17
3. Acts 23:11
4. Philippians 1:21 (NIV)
5. Acts 27:24
6. Acts 27:22 (NIV)
7. Acts 27:22
8. Acts 25:25
9. Isaiah 19:21
10. Romans 1:8 (NIV)
11. Acts 28:15

6.05 – Running to Embrace

On the brink of Paul's showdown with Caesar, the narrative on the Headquarters' floor draws tantalisingly to a halt. Did Paul ever receive his chance to speak about Jesus? It does not say. Phase Six seems to finish incomplete.

A few annotations, however, hint toward the failure of Paul's ambition. Within five years of Paul's arrival, it says that the Jesus advocates started to be persecuted throughout Rome. In the name of entertainment, Emperor Nero began burning these 'Christians' at his parties.

And for the next two and a half centuries, persecution persisted.

Christians made for excellent entertainment in the Colosseum. Mauled by gladiators and lions, their deaths were cheered by ecstatic sell-out crowds.

But then.

Quite remarkably.

Perhaps even miraculously.

Our heart is leaping at the revelation.

Emperor Constantine, ruler of the entire Roman Empire, declared himself a Christian. And from that day on, Jesus' radical teachings - where all human lives were precious and valuable - began to transform the Empire's heart.

Change hardly occurred overnight. The annotations

point out that for at least the next one hundred years, 'Christian' Emperors continued to sponsor gruesome gladiator battles.

But eventually... eventually the horrifying gladiator contests were seen as just that: horrifying.

Kneeling on the Headquarters' floor, our eyes open in relief and delight.

This was heaven invading earth.

A new world was being born.

A new creation was blossoming.

'Whom can I send? Who will go for us?'[1]

We freeze. The voice is with us, close to us, coming from behind us.

There is no fear within us. We feel at peace, excited, expectant, completely at ease in our own skin; and moving slowly, like a bride processing down the aisle, we rise and rotate, savouring every second of anticipation.

His arms are muscular, his chin stubbled, his eyes dark and glistening. Never before have we felt so alive, so at home, so complete, so ecstatic; we are staring into the dark glistening eyes of Jesus.

And without thinking, we are sprinting, sprinting, sprinting... running to embrace.

With arms open wide, Jesus intercepts our stride and swings us round. Then draws us close.

'Oh, how I've longed for this moment,' he whispers as we bury our head into his chest.

We are lost in his arms.

Time has stopped.

There is nowhere else we'd rather be.

We.

Are.

Lost.

In.

The.

Arms.

Of.

Love.

Time returns with a jolt when our right thumb connects with a hole in Jesus' wrist.

Ashamed, our head bows away.

'But... but... but why?' we ask.

'Because *I love you with a love that lasts forever*;[2] because *the greatest love a person can show is to die for his friends*;[3] because I knit you together in your mother's womb, planning your days before you were born, desiring only the best for you, my child.'[4]

Our eyes close in surrender, allowing Ruach to take hold of Jesus' words and embed them at the core of our being.

Suddenly a thought stuns us cold: are we dead?

After all, this is... Jesus.

We blurt out the question.

'Not quite,' smiles Jesus. 'But that fall from the loft did hit you hard. You'll regain consciousness soon.'

Time freezes again before our thoughts explode into a thousand frenzied directions. Again we are lost. Uprooted. No longer at home.

From amongst a multitude of sensations, we gradually

distinguish cool invigorating water being poured over our feet. We look down to see Jesus kneeling before us holding a wooden bowl, a towel draped over his shoulder. Our socks and shoes have been removed.

'Ruach, Abba, and I have been revealing our story of love to you. What you have experienced in this room, these were just the headlines, the highlights. There is so much more to discover and discuss.'

Jesus appears calm, seemingly unperturbed by our shock.

'The Son of Man did not come to be served. He came to serve others and to give his life as a ransom for many.[5] *I, your Lord and Teacher, have washed your feet.*[6] Now I invite you to do the same for others. I invite you to play your part in completing Phase Six.'

Jesus rubs our feet back and forth in a simple harmonic motion.

'Accept others as I have accepted you.[7] Forgive as I have forgiven you.'

We nod, taking it all in. Jesus is wringing out his towel, squeezing every last filthy drip back into the bowl.

'Ruach, Abba and I do *not want anyone to be lost, but* desire *all people to change their hearts and lives.*[8] *Let your light shine, so all may see your good deeds and praise your Father in heaven.*[9] *Be holy because I am holy.'*[10]

'But... but...' we start to protest, taken aback by the extremity of Jesus' words.

'Our breath will help you shine,' Jesus cuts across, realising our fear of inadequacy. 'We will be with you.'

With our hand in his, Jesus pushes himself up by his

knees.

'You can have peace in me. In this world you will have trouble, but be brave! I have defeated the world.'[11]

As his voice rises climatically, Jesus turns to the Phase Five wall and starts to peel down the posters. Hidden beneath, he reveals a dull grey door.

At first we are wooed by a sumptuous perfume, then as the door opens further, a bright, diverse, wonderfully kept garden visually delights. The complete sensory experience takes our breath away.

'The Good News about God's Kingdom will be preached in all the world, to every nation. Then the end will come.'[12]

Jesus turns to us and smiles. He signals for us to follow, then steps out into the gorgeously fresh expanse.

'Come, let's go and meet Abba.

'He will take great delight in you.

'He will quiet you with his love.

'He will rejoice over you with singing.[13]

'And you will find him with arms open wide, running to embrace.'[14]

1. Isaiah 6:8
2. Jeremiah 31:3
3. John 15:13
4. Psalm 139:14–16
5. Matthew 20:28
6. John 13:14
7. Romans 15:7
8. 2 Peter 3:9
9. Matthew 5:16
10. Leviticus 19:2
11. John 16:33
12. Matthew 24:14
13. Zephaniah 3:17 (NIV)
14. Luke 15:20

PHASE SEVEN

7.00 – Breath is Stolen

Old age plays tricks on the mind. Time becomes distorted. Memories present themselves as if they are present realities.

Repulsive.

Haunting.

Spine-chilling memories.

First there's the murder of every one of his friends. Paul was beheaded. Peter was crucified - upside down. Then there's the demolition of Jerusalem: smoke billowing from smouldering ruins, corpses rotting under rubble.

Those caught fleeing the annihilation were strung up on Jerusalem's outskirts, arms swept across a horizontal wooden beam, legs draped down the vertical. The Romans could execute up to five hundred a day.

John's eyes glaze over.

Oh Jesus, beautiful Jesus: he foresaw Jerusalem's devastation;[1] this was the inevitable fate of a city which dared to challenge the Empire.

Oh Jesus, precious Jesus. John is head over heels, besotted, in love with Love.[2] And Love *is patient*, Love *is kind*. Love *does not envy...* Love *keeps no record of wrongs.* Love… Love…

Oh Jesus, stunning Jesus: *Love never fails.*[3] John's suffering persists, his memories haunt, but John has no fear; *God's perfect love drives out fear.*[4]

Oh Jesus, sensational Jesus. There he is: the Son of Man travelling on the clouds of heaven.[5] There he is: eyes blazing like fire, hair *white as snow.*[6]

In reality, John is in a dark cave on a remote island.

In his mind, he is in heaven.

Wave after wave of sumptuous harmonies wash over John. Lightning flashes, thunder cracks,[7] an emerald rainbow encircles Elohim's throne,[8] bizarre creatures of every shape and size fill the room.

John's heart is on the brink of explosion.

His eyes are transfixed upon a lamb.

A lamb in the centre of the throne.

The lamb is slain.[9]

Yet clearly alive.

'Because you were killed,' the crowds sing, *'with the blood of your death you bought people for God from every tribe, language, people and nation.*[10] *The Lion from the tribe of Judah, David's descendant, has won the victory.'*[11]

John looks on in adoration and awe. Possessing the power of a lion, Jesus offered himself as a lamb. This is a defining image of Love - beautiful self-sacrificing Love. The image is a rallying cry to those still suffering under the persecution of Emperor Domitian.

To all who endure.

To all who persevere.

To all *who overcome.*[12]

To all *who win the victory*.

Jesus promises, 'You *will never be hungry or thirsty again*.[13] You *will sit with me on my throne*,[14] possessing *power over the nations*.[15] You will dwell in the *New Jerusalem*,[16] surrounded by the presence of God.'[17]

John's mind trips and jolts.

Cheers turn to screams.

Flames rise and engulf.

A burning lake of sulphur stretches out before John's eyes. Its stench is grotesque, putrid, absolutely rancid, and John instantly masks his face, peering out through clenched fingers.

From the very beginning of Love's Rescue Mission, the Hijacker has been crushed on the head, destined for defeat. Yet evil has continued to bite back, clinging to the heel, refusing to let go.[18]

There can be no paradise until all evil is eliminated.

All injustice: eradicated.

All bloodshed: abolished.

All discrimination: demolished.

No more majorities manipulating minorities.

No more corruption profiting the powerful.

No more disease, no more death.

Death must die.[19]

The Hijacker lets out a searing satanic scream as his clinging grip gives way, and the master of darkness slips and falls *into the lake of burning sulphur*. Flailing in the flames, there he will be *punished day and night for ever and ever*,[20] never to contaminate, capture, conquer, control - never to hijack - a precious human life ever again.

Love, by its very nature, demands justice.

And here, in the burning flames, justice is done.

Howling in agony, the Hijacker reaches out a hand and in one final evil act, grabs hold of a chain of captives and drags them down with him.

Drowning in a cesspit of hatred, Love's precious children...

Breathe.

Out.

For.

The.

Final.

Time.

Tears cascade incessantly from the bloodshot, pain-stained eyes of three friends huddled together. Mourning their loss, with arms wrapped around each other, the Community of Elohim weep and grieve with every essence of their being. With their offer of rescue continuously rejected, there is nothing more that can be done.

Love's masterpieces have erased their names from the book of life.[21]

They have chosen death.

Writhing in agony, John fights to shut down his mind. He lies rigid on the ground, hands clawing over his eyes, his whole body crying out for all to choose life.

Ruach holds Yeshua in a tight intimate embrace. *'Those who win the victory,'* she caresses, *'will not be hurt by the second death.*[22] *I will not erase their names from the book of life.'*[23]

'I am going to attract her,' weeps Yeshua. '*I will lead her into the desert and speak tenderly to her. There I will give her back her vineyards and I will make the Valley of Trouble a door of hope. There she will respond as when she was young, as when she came out of Egypt.'*[24]

Ruach rises, shimmering with delight. 'Look, my love, *who is this coming out of the desert, leaning on her lover?'*[25]

Looking over his shoulder, the Groom's breath is stolen. There in the distance, emerging from the desert - dressed in white *fine linen*[26] and leaning on Abba's arm - Jesus' Bride glides gracefully towards him.

1. Luke 21:24
2. 1 John 4:16
3. 1 Corinthians 13:4-8 (NIV)
4. 1 John 4:18
5. Revelation 1:12
6. Revelation 1:14
7. Revelation 4:5
8. Revelation 4:3
9. Revelation 5:6
10. Revelation 5:9
11. Revelation 5:5
12. Revelation 3:21 (NIV)
13. Revelation 2:17 & 7:16
14. Revelation 3:21
15. Revelation 2:26
16. Revelation 3:12
17. Revelation 7:15
18. Genesis 3:15
19. Revelation 20:14
20. Revelation 20:10
21. Revelation 20:15
22. Revelation 2:11
23. Revelation 3:5
24. Hosea 2:14-15
25. Song of Songs 8:5
26. Revelation 19:8

7.01 – Every Desire is Found

In the beginning,
The first humans had a choice.
It was a choice between two trees.

One tree was
Called
Life.

Fruit from the
Other tree
Brought
Death.

Choose Life…
Choose Life…
Choose Life…

The first humans did not choose Life.

The family of Abraham,
The people of Israel
Were slaves
In Egypt.
And as slaves.
They were hurting.
Bleeding.
Suffering.
They were crying out in agony.

When Yahweh heard their cries.
And pulled them out of Egypt.
With Moses' help,
Yahweh led them
To the brink
Of paradise.
A land with rivers
And pools of water,
With springs that flow
In the valleys and hills.
With *wheat and barley,*
Vines, fig trees, pomegranates,
Olive oil and honey.
A land with everything
They would ever need.[1]

And poised on the brink of paradise
The Israelites were given a choice.
A choice between life and death,
Between blessings and curses.
And Moses begged,
Moses pleaded: *'Now, choose life!'*[2]

Choose Life...

Choose Life…

Choose Life…

Jesus said, *'I have come*
That they may have life,
And have it to the full.'[3]

But Jesus was captured.
Jesus was tied to a tree.
And on that tree Jesus hurt.
Jesus bled.
Jesus suffered.
Jesus cried out.
In excruciating agony.

On that tree Jesus died.

The one who had said he had come to bring life.

He died.

But after two nights of
Jesus' dead body
Lying buried
In the ground,

Life burst forth from the grave.
Jesus defeated death.
Once and for all.
Leaving Life,
Life in all its fullness,
Reigning victorious.
Jesus *took away the curse* of *the law.*[4]
Now only blessing remains.

Choose Life…
Choose Life…
Choose Life…

Dressed in white *fine linen,*
Bright and clean,[5]
Jesus' Bride glides gracefully towards him.
She is gorgeous and elegant,
Perfectly pure,
Without spot or wrinkle,
Holy and without blemish.[6]

Wrapping his right arm around her waist,
Placing his left hand under her head,[7]
Yeshua holds his Bride in romantic intimacy.

'My love, you are full of delights.[8]
My bride, you have thrilled my heart.[9]
My bride, your lips drip honey.[10]
How beautiful you are, my darling!
Oh, you are beautiful!
Your eyes behind your veil are like doves.[11]
My darling, everything about you is beautiful,
There is nothing wrong with you.'[12]

'You are so handsome, my lover.[13]
Your *mouth is sweet to kiss,*
I desire you so *very much.*
You are *my lover and my friend.*[14]
You have *brought me to* your *banquet room,*
Your *banner over me is love.*[15]
I belong to you *my lover*
And my lover belongs to me.[16]
I belong to you *my lover*
And you desire only me.'[17]

Gazing far into his Bride's eyes,
Jesus tenderly makes his vows:
'My darling, I *will wipe away*
Every tear from your *eyes.*
There will be no more death,
Or mourning,
Or crying,
Or pain,
For the old order of things has passed away.[18]
My darling, look, *I am making all things new!'*[19]

A standing ovation
And deafening applause
Greets the kiss of Husband and Wife
As a *new Jerusalem* comes *down*
Out of heaven from God.[20]

'*Arise, my darling, my beautiful one,*
And come with me.[21]
Look, the winter is past;
The rains are over and gone.
Blossoms appear through all the land.
The time has come to sing.'[22]

Walking hand in hand,
Husband and Wife step
Into a panorama of paradise.
Every flower is in bloom.
Every crop bears fruit.
Every creature lives in harmony.
Even *wolves and lambs eat together in peace.*[23]

Here in paradise,
Husband and Wife
Dwell forever
In intimacy together.

Full of joy, there is no pain.
Full of love, there is no shame.
Full of Life, there is no Death.

The first humans were born into a similar paradise.
Sharing the creative character of their creator,
    Humans built upon the lush green landscape.
        Some constructions were oppressive.
           Stifling and damaging.
       Others were objects of beauty.
      Others brought order and structure,
     Enabling large populations
    To live together in community.
And here in the new creation,
Elohim takes the work of human hands,
And transforms it into paradise.

In New Jerusalem,
Husband and Wife walk lost in each other's arms,
Gazing at a city *decorated with every kind of jewel*,[24]
Marvelling at a street of *pure gold as clear as glass*.[25]

In New Jerusalem,
The city gates are named after Israel's twelve tribes,[26]
The foundation stones commemorate Jesus' disciples.[27]

In New Jerusalem,
Every covenant finds fulfilment.
The new creation begun with Noah,
The blessing of all people, promised to Abraham,
The full blessing of the law, presented to Moses,
The everlasting kingdom, ruled by David's descendant,
It is all present, all made possible by Jesus.[28]

In New Jerusalem,
There is no need for a Temple.
Yahweh's Shekinah is everywhere.
God's presence is with his people.[29]
Ruach inhabits every life.

In New Jerusalem,
The sun is superfluous.
For *the glory of God is its light.*[30]
It will never be night again.[31]
For *God is light, and in him*
There is no darkness.[32]

In New Jerusalem,
A river *shining like crystals,*[33]
Gushes down from Yahweh's throne.
'Let whoever is thirsty come,'[34] Yeshua ushers.
'Whoever wishes may have the water of life
As a free gift.'[35]

Because Love has paid the price.
Victory is free.

'To those who win the victory,'
Jesus cheers, effervescent with joy,
'I will give the right to eat the fruit
From the tree of life.'[36]

From the beginning to the new beginning,
Every human has had a choice.
It was a choice between two trees.

In New Jerusalem,
There is only one tree.
Life: it has been chosen.

Abba takes the hand of Yeshua on his right and Ruach
on his left.
Locked in embrace, the view electrifies Elohim's heart.
Everywhere they look, their every desire is found.
With justice realised, their character surrounds.
With beauty restored, their creativity abounds.
With intimacy chosen, relationship resounds.
Love beams with a great satisfied smile.
The Rescue Mission is complete.

1. Deuteronomy 8:7-9
2. Deuteronomy 30:19
3. John 10:10 (NIV)
4. Galatians 3:13
5. Revelation 19:8
6. Ephesians 5:25-27 (NIV)
7. Song of Songs 2:6
8. Song of Songs 7:6
9. Song of Songs 4:9
10. Song of Songs 4:11
11. Song of Songs 4:1
12. Song of Songs 4:7
13. Song of Songs 1:16
14. Song of Songs 5:16
15. Song of Songs 2:4
16. Song of Songs 6:3
17. Song of Songs 7:10
18. Revelation 21:4 (NIV)
19. Revelation 21:5
20. Revelation 21:2
21. Song of Songs 2:10 (NIV)
22. Song of Songs 2:11-12
23. Isaiah 65:25
24. Revelation 21:19
25. Revelation 21:21
26. Revelation 21:12
27. Revelation 21:14
28. 2 Corinthians 1:20
29. Revelation 21:3
30. Revelation 21:23
31. Revelation 22:5
32. 1 John 1:5
33. Revelation 22:1
34. Revelation 21:6-7
35. Revelation 22:17
36. Revelation 2:7

Pete Atkinson is a secondary teacher with MA and MEd degrees from Cambridge University. He is married with two young children.

Writing The Rescue Mission was a labour of love over 15 years. Pete is grateful for numerous supporters but he is especially indebted to Rachel Smith for relentlessly enduring an onslaught of early drafts.

Printed in Great Britain
by Amazon

39314501R00147